O Wow!

O Wow!

Discovering Your Ultimate Orgasm

by Jenny Block

Foreword by Betty Dodson

PRESS

Published in the United States by Cleis Press,
an imprint of Start Midnight, LLC,
101 Hudson Street, 37th Floor, Suite 3705, Jersey City, NJ 07302.

Printed in the United States.
Cover design: Scott Idleman/Blink
Cover photograph: iStockphoto
Text design: Frank Wiedemann

First Edition.
10 9 8 7 6 5 4 3 2 1

Trade paper ISBN: 978-1-62778-146-6
E-book ISBN: 979-1-62778-148-0

Library of Congress Cataloging-in-Publication Data is available.

For Lacey

The sexual hunger of the female, and her capacity for copulation completely exceeds that of any male.... To all intents and purposes, the human female is sexually insatiable...

—Mary Jane Sherfey,
The Nature and Evolution of Female Sexuality

It cannot be denied that the design of the human female's reproductive system is far from what the standard narrative predicts, and thus demands radical rethinking of the evolution of female sexuality.

—Christopher Ryan and Cacilda Jethá,
Sex at Dawn: The Prehistoric Origins of Modern Sexuality

Contents

Foreword
Betty Dodson

WHEN CARLIN, MY BUSINESS PARTNER, told me she wanted to add another woman to our already full Bodysex workshop, I complained as usual. It's a lot easier to run a smaller group because I can keep track of the women in the circle much more easily. Aesthetically, it's more pleasing, and, I'll admit, I've become a bit rigid in my old age.

Carlin urged me to allow Jenny into the circle because Jenny was writing a book about women's orgasms. She went on to explain that Jenny was one of the few young women blogging for the *Huffington Post* about sex. My first thought was that she was most likely a spoiled brat with a rich daddy who had made a sizable donation to our foundation.

As it happened, Jenny was adorable, extremely smart, and, although she remains married to a man and is a mother, she thoroughly enjoys sex with women and identifies as a lesbian. So, I had to admit, what's not to love?

Although I've done these workshops off and on for forty-some years, I'm always experimenting. So nothing is etched in stone. With this one, I announced that during our erotic recess, when everyone focuses on having as many orgasms as they desire, any woman wanting personal attention could just raise her hand and I would pull up alongside. I've done this before, and while it takes a lot more energy, I also know it's very effective.

Forty minutes into the masturbation ritual, Jenny raised her hand. She was on the opposite side of the circle, and since I'm into conserving my energy, I simply crawled across the room on my hands and knees.

As I sat alongside Jenny, I immediately saw her problem. As she got close to orgasm, she arched her back. Wilhelm Reich referred to this as the "Hysterical Arch," an unconscious response to control strong sexual sensations. I became aware of this pattern during sex parties in the '60s. Back then, I simply observed and said nothing unless I knew the woman very well.

With Jenny, I placed my hand just above her pubic mound and pressed down firmly using my weight. Then I began moving the Vaginal Barbell to get her pelvic thrusting to match her breathing, which I modeled by breathing out loud. Then I moved my hand and made a fist to apply pressure to her perineum.

When I saw she was right in front of an orgasm, instead of moving along to the next woman, I stayed with her to make sure she came for the sake of her book. Jenny was so happy; she immediately assisted the woman across the circle from her. *Perfect,* I thought. That's how the sisterhood spreads from woman to woman.

Although this might sound wild or far out to many, it's actually similar to having a dance instructor take you in her arms to perform the steps with you. However, because I'm dealing with sex, everyone puts far more scrutiny on it rather than seeing it as a regular, everyday activity. In this way, we make sex seem shocking. After all these years, I'm very aware of what's happening on several levels: the individual woman, the group, and my role as facilitator. While I treat this seriously as a teacher, I do so in a casual manner, often using humor to help normalize whatever sexual activity is taking place.

Because the workshops are a group activity, I didn't spend any alone time with Jenny. Since Carlin organizes the groups, she's the one who deals with each woman and has individual contact with them via email. When Carlin said Jenny was going to write up her experience for the *Huffington Post,* I groaned inwardly—so few reporters ever manage to get the essence of a Bodysex workshop. It's usually underreported or sensationalized.

When I read Jenny's review, I loved it. She seemed so young to be such an accurate observer and experienced reporter of what took place. Both Carlin and I agreed that it was one of the best workshop write-ups we'd ever gotten. Also, it unleashed a rash of publicity, and our numbers soared. That's when I question why I bother to sound like Greta Garbo—

"I want to be left alone." What I really mean is, "Stop bothering me while I answer more questions from kids around the world"—my current obsession. After all, we are in the business of sharing positive sex information for girls and women, boys and men from around the world. So why wouldn't I welcome publicity?

Before finishing this current book, Jenny sent her first one: *Open: Love, Sex, and Life in an Open Marriage*. So I read it before this newest one. I liked the comment on the flap: "*Open* challenges our notions of what traditional marriage looks like, and presents one woman's journey down an uncertain path that ultimately proves that open marriage is a viable option—and one that's in fact better for some couples than conventional marriage." When I received her most recent book, *O Wow! Discovering Your Ultimate Orgasm,* it was every bit as honest.

I am very impressed with this young woman's personal honesty and ability to experience, as well as research and then report back to her readers in a very clear, organized manner. The experiences of this brave, outspoken young woman mirrored my sexual explorations during America's sexual revolution in the late '60s and early '70s.

At the time, we were a handful of "freaks" who were openly sharing our orgasms and exploring what non-monogamy might look like. This was happening in a world that fiercely came in twos, like Noah's Ark. For women, faking orgasms was seen as simply having good manners. Back then, we were concerned about protecting a man's ego even if it meant sacrificing our own.

Then I got it! Jenny is one of my spiritual daughters. More accurately, she is my spiritual granddaughter. We have traveled similar paths searching for sexual equality, fulfillment, and happiness. First with ourselves! Then we can pass this information and knowledge on to our friends and lovers. I welcome Jenny to the sisterhood of sex-positive feminist warriors who are creating a path for our sisters, daughters, and mothers to follow, paved with the knowledge that sexual pleasure and orgasms are not only our birthright, but the basis for our social, physical, and spiritual healing.

I

Decoding Female Orgasm

Revolution

IT'S TIME FOR A REVOLUTION of the orgasmic kind. It's time for every woman to embark on a search for her ultimate orgasm. It's going to be the most pleasurable and the most powerful revolution yet. Women who regularly experience ultimate orgasms have the power to change, well, everything. It's the easiest, most delicious proposition ever. All we have to do is come.

The idea for this revolution came from a painful and entirely unscientific experiment: I came and then I didn't. That is, I had sex and enjoyed orgasms—with a partner and without. And I refrained from having sex and denied myself orgasms—with a partner and with myself. Sounds simple, I know. But it's bigger than it sounds, because it's about coming, and yet it isn't. It's about denial and satisfaction, and it's about what happens to our bodies, minds, and spirits when we withhold versus when we give in to release.

Without orgasm, I am tired and in pain. I am lethargic and unmotivated. My creativity is as a dried well. I am closed, quick to lose hope and even quicker to temper. With orgasm, well, it's the opposite all around.

Women are overburdened, overstressed, overworked, and underpaid.

I wish we could turn all of that around in one day. Equal pay. Equal protection. Equal everything all around.

But I'm a realist, and I know that isn't going to happen overnight. Gloria Steinem, Audre Lorde, Adrienne Rich, Camille Paglia, and so many others have been fighting the good fight and writing the right words for generations, and although we have come miraculously far, we are still woefully behind.

I have discovered a crack in the wall, though. I have uncovered one space where our inequality is evident and from which we can derive great power—female orgasm. It is both concrete and metaphorical. If we owned it and harnessed it and made it our own, we could almost certainly turn things around overnight.

Orgasm is the base of all female power. Detach from it and we literally repress ourselves, our power, and our ability to rise. Connect to it and we are a force to be reckoned with, the likes of which no one has ever seen.

To do that, we first must ask: Why has female orgasm been relegated to the shadows for so long?

1. It empowers women.

It's a sad fact of life: Things that empower women often get quashed and squashed and stamped on and out. Voting. Revealing bathing suits. Abortion. Birth control. Need I go on? If women are in control of their orgasms, they don't need men. They can still want them. But they don't need them to "make" them come. Being in control of your own orgasm is liberation to the nth degree.

2. It involves admitting that the female body is equal to—or better than—a man's.

If female orgasm is as important as male orgasm, then the female body is as good as the male body, which means—gasp—women themselves are just as important. Because women don't generally orgasm from the act that causes procreation, women's pleasure has taken a backseat to men's and women, all too often, have taken a backseat to men. It's time for us to be in the driver's seat.

3. Men don't understand it.

No matter how much you study or read or experiment in the field, if you can't *have* a female orgasm, you can never truly understand female orgasm. You can learn the mechanics. You can hear the explanations. But only a woman can tell you how female orgasm feels—and even then, she can only tell you how it feels for her.

4. It's not easy or instant or simple.

Female orgasm is not quick, and male orgasm often is. Female orgasm is not simple, and male orgasm often is. We live in a male-centric world. Ground zero is always the male experience. That is the problem when it comes to female orgasm: It's judged against male orgasm, and that simply doesn't make any sense. When it comes to female orgasm, the only ground zero is the woman having that orgasm.

5. It seems selfish to worry about it.

Women have been made to believe that female orgasm is superfluous. That it's extra. That it's a #firstworldproblem. Male orgasm is coddled and revered and covered by health insurance. Female orgasm is ridiculed and pooh-poohed. Women who care about it are selfish whores. Good girls lie back and say, "Thank you. That felt very nice." And don't tell their partners what it is that they actually desire.

6. It's sexual and women aren't supposed to be sexual—or, if they are, it has to be for men.

Women are sexual. Men are sexual and women are sexual. Women's sexuality is not founded in or based on male sexuality. It does not exist for men. It exists very happily without men. Women can choose to share their sexuality with men, but they get to choose and define what that means and how that looks. Otherwise, what on earth is the point? If you're not trying to make a baby, why have intercourse with a man who doesn't make you come? If you want closeness, cuddle. If you want romance, have a candlelit dinner. If you want intimacy, take a long, hot bubble bath together. But why have intercourse so that he can come and you can lie in bed awake with blue box?[1] That simply makes no sense, and it's time for this nonsense to stop.

7. It doesn't require a man, and actually does better without the penis and its needs and demands.

Those buggers can be very insistent, as anyone who has been with one sexually knows! In general, men don't do well when they aren't needed. But it's time to shift the paradigm to one of want and desire, rather than one of need.

A woman does not need access to a penis to have an orgasm. In fact, the needs of the penis often hinder a woman in pursuit of an orgasm. That is threatening to men. And that is a reason for the powers that be to belittle female orgasm and keep it in its place.

8. We've made it all about power.

It's a shame. But it's true. "I can make you come" has become a badge of honor, and it puts pressure on the woman to come and pressure on the person that woman is with to make her come. The only power should lie with the woman having the orgasm. She has the power to have it and the power to direct how she wants to have it. No other power should be at play.

9. It's neglected by science (because it has to do with women).

Insurance covers Viagra but not vibrators. Male sex drive and impotence are studied ad nauseam. But no comparable research is done on women. In fact, female sexuality is so poorly understood by the general public, that a massive majority of women still refer to their vulvas as vaginas. This isn't just about sex. It's about anything when it comes to women and science. Men are ground zero. The test case. The basis. And it just doesn't work when it comes to orgasm (or to most things for that matter).

---

1   The female equivalent of blue balls. Special thanks to my sister, Rebecca Block, for helping me coin that.

10. It isn't required for reproduction.

Although some doctors will tell you that it can help, female orgasm isn't actually required in order to create a baby. But if making babies is the only reason for intercourse, then you might as well have men ejaculate in a cup and women artificially inseminated.

Intercourse is about pleasure—primarily men's pleasure. So it doesn't matter if female orgasms don't play a part in procreation. If a woman is going to give a man pleasure by allowing—yes, allowing—him to enter her body, then her pleasure should hold equal weight. It's not extra. It's not, "Do you want me to do you now?" Sex is not sex if the pleasure of both parties is not equally weighted. It's male masturbation with the woman playing the role of masturbation sleeve.

11. It doesn't stop the world from turning if it doesn't happen— although maybe it should.

It's too bad the world isn't powered by female orgasm, the way it is by screams in *Monsters, Inc.* But because the world goes on whether or not women have orgasms, we don't give female orgasm the stature it deserves. The truth is that the world would be a much better place, a happier, stronger, more gender-balanced place, if female orgasm was prized in the same way as male orgasm. That's why giving it props is so very important.

In other words, the treatment of female orgasm is all about socialization. The only way forward is to reorient. This isn't one of those revolutions that requires legislation or lobbying or even marching in the streets. All it requires is for women to decide that they are going to be responsible for their own orgasms and to commit to having them, because they are a right and a benefit to society no matter how you cut it.

Now this is about far more than finding the right position, or even trying certain positions for the sake of trying them. This is about finding your orgasm, your best orgasm, your ultimate orgasm. It's about letting go of everything you've heard or been taught and instead trusting the body you have and what it desires.

What is an ultimate orgasm?

An ultimate orgasm is your personal best orgasm. It doesn't leave anything on the table. It doesn't want anything more. It lasts as long as it lasts. It takes as long as it takes. It's as loud and messy or as quiet and tidy as you like. It has no room for shame or apology. It leaves you feeling like you just landed on another planet, and you definitely need to take some time before you can drive a motor vehicle or operate heavy machinery.

An ultimate orgasm comes from questioning, exploring, experimenting, taking every chance, making every turn, and looking under every rock to figure out what feels best to you, with no concern for how society or religion or anything else defines sex or sexuality or female orgasm. The ultimate orgasm belongs to you and only you, and it is your responsibility to find it, to have it, and to keep it for as long as you want to live a fully actualized, fully orgasmic, fully sexually satisfying life.

Want to know the secret to having the ultimate orgasm? Knowing your body and being in the zone. That's it. Lots of tips and tricks and ideas to follow later. But first and foremost, we have to empower ourselves to feel pleasure.

"Knowledge is power," as the old *Schoolhouse Rock* adage goes. You can stumble upon an orgasm, sure. But in general, amazing, consistent, ultimate orgasms come from knowing what works, being in the moment, and advocating for your orgasm. No matter how much your partner adores you and is committed to your orgasm, ultimately you are the only one who can and should be responsible for it.

By the same token, when it comes to information, sometimes too much can be a bad thing. Let me assure you—you're not doing it wrong. There aren't just "Ten Perfect Positions" or "Eight Ways to Orgasm" or whatever the magazines tell you. What your body desires is right, is good, is perfect—and anyone who tells you otherwise is a lousy partner. Period.

Orgasm isn't easy. It isn't automatic. It isn't something some people are good at and some people are bad at. Sure, some people might be born with some innate talent. But, in general, it's like everything else. You have to practice. You have to commit. You have to focus. And you have to put in the time. You'll get better at it, and it will come easier. And it'll be worth it.

And, with any luck, it'll change the world too.

Your Big O

This book is about finding your ultimate orgasm. Not *the* orgasm or *an* orgasm, but *your* ultimate orgasm. Finding what suits you perfectly. Maybe you have one. Maybe you have several. Maybe you have one now but have the potential to have several others.

The thing is, too many women don't have one at all. Or rather, they're not regularly enjoying their personal orgasm best, the one that makes their toes curl and their breath stop and their body melt and their mind go interplanetary. Their ultimate orgasm.

And if you're wondering, yes, there are orgasms like that, and yes, you may be able to have one. The trick is letting go of all of your preconceived notions, all of your hang-ups and baggage and worries. The trick is to stop reading those articles that make female orgasm seem like a party trick for male pleasure, step away from the porn as comparison or education, and, perhaps most importantly, stop comparing female orgasm to male orgasm.

You have only one goal: to find your personal orgasm best. Maybe it comes from partner sex. Maybe from masturbation. Maybe from a combination. Maybe it stems from your brain. Or maybe your skin. Or maybe deep inside you. It makes no difference. There's no judgment. No right or wrong way. No bad orgasms.

My guess is that for most women, the ultimate orgasm is the blended orgasm, the one that comes from direct stimulation of the external bud of the clitoris in combination with any number of other activities in other zones I'll address throughout this book.

(Time out—The next time you masturbate or have sex, take note of whether or not you orgasm, the strength of that orgasm, and what you were doing when you came. I'll bet, if it was a knock-out one, it was blended.)

There are several steps in the journey to discovering your ultimate orgasm. You might be well on your way, or reading this book might be your very first step. It makes no difference. The only thing that matters is that you've decided to read this book and take this journey to find your personal best, your ultimate orgasm, no matter what that is or how you get there.

We'll start with the orgasm basics. We'll explore the health benefits. We'll dispel some myths. We'll cover the steps to take in pursuit of a great orgasm. We'll talk about all of the different zones from which an ultimate orgasm can emanate, including your skin. (Yup. Your skin. More on that later...)

The truth is, an orgasm is an orgasm. The differences from one orgasm to another reside in how you get there and what feels best to you. That's what this book is all about—discovering what your personal orgasm best is and finding your ultimate orgasm.

Remember, orgasm is the center of women's power. So tapping into yours is key to tapping into success in every aspect of your life.

This book is about being in the trenches. There's plenty of science out there about orgasm. But this book is about the O. Not the science. Not the theory. The actual experience. This book is rooted in my personal experience.

It's about all of the books and articles I read, from Freud to Kinsey and from Christopher Ryan to Felice Newman, and all of the experts with whom I spoke, from Betty Dodson to Dr. Justin R. Garcia. It's about my survey of nearly 150 women, that asked them what sex and orgasm meant and felt like and looked like to them.

And, as I mentioned above, I did a little, incredibly unscientific experiment. I went without coming for a couple of weeks. And you know what? I felt lousy. Then I made sure I came every single day, and lo and behold, all things were right with the world again.

I also started having some really stellar sex. The "let's give ourselves over completely, see what really works, and leave the shame at the door" kind of sex. I did all the things and tried all the stuff, and I even went to a workshop to learn from the master. (More about that in Chapter Two.)

I'll talk about my own sexual history later, but for now, it seems important at least to mention that for many years, I had sex with men. Some of it was very good. Very, very good, in fact. And a lot of it was mediocre. I now identify as a lesbian, and so, for some time now, I have only been having sex with women. And in the middle of all of my research—both field and academic—I had a revelation. Women haven't really had much say in how sex and desire and pleasure are defined. It has been handed down to them—by men—and it's antithetical to the truth of women's sexuality and their bodies.

I have no interest in laying any blame here, but our current cultural climate combined with popularly held religious beliefs "that have no business in the bedroom" have been very damaging when it comes to women's roles and men's roles and the definition of sex. Movies with a man climbing on top of a woman and thrusting sexily while she moans, both of them collapsing three minutes later, haven't helped matters.

Great orgasms, ultimate orgasms, require commitment from all parties involved. I'll say it now and I'll say it again. There are all sorts of exceptions out there. There are men who don't care as much about their own orgasms as they do about their partner's. There are women who can come just from a penis being slipped into their vagina. There are as many types of sexual desires and interests and patterns as there are stars in the sky.

But if you are a woman who wants to discover her ultimate orgasm, or a person of any gender who wants to facilitate women's orgasms, then we have to talk about the most common situation. And that's what I've described in this book. No room for ego. If you're the partner for which nothing in this book comes as a surprise, good on you. You're in great shape. But if not, fear not; we only know what we know. We only learn what we have seen and experienced.

We've all been led astray when it comes to female orgasm. The good news is that there's no time like the present to make the past the past and set things right.

The Science of Orgasm

Here's the problem—we're having procreative sex for recreation. We need to be having recreational sex.

It's interesting. Lesbian sex has been so dreadfully marginalized for so long because it goes against the procreative model of sex that so many of us grew up with. But the truth is, the best way to open up our vision of what sex can look like is to model it after lesbian sex, where there are no rules or guidelines or preconceived notions. No guidelines means more possibilities. Lots and lots of possibilities.

I remember the very first time I was with a woman, I was fascinated by the way we followed the pleasure instead of the directions. There was no one way or one thing or one act. There was no beginning or end. There was nothing but "This feels good! Does that feel good?" until we both passed out from giddy exhaustion.

That is how sex should be regardless of the genders of the people in play.

Famed sex researcher Dr. Beverly Whipple, the woman responsible for coining the name "G-spot," refers to this as pleasure-oriented as opposed to goal-oriented sex.

"I look at sexuality as being pleasure-directed and not goal-directed," Whipple told me when we chatted over the phone about this project. "For goal-directed, I use the analogy of the staircase with the big O from penile intercourse.

"Pleasure-directed is a circle. Sometimes holding hands is what we want. Sometimes oral sex. We enjoy what it is that we enjoy. It's very important for people to be aware of what they like, and to acknowledge it and communicate it.

"There are many, many ways we can enjoy sexual pleasure. There is so much for women to enjoy, and it's time we focus on women and what feels good to them. We have to stop trying to put women in the male, linear model."

I love Whipple's illustrations of the goal-directed (staircase) and plea-sure-directed (circle) models of sex.

Sexual Experiences

GOAL-DIRECTED

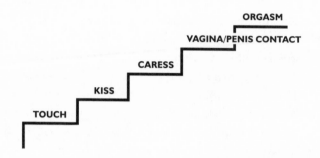

PLEASURE-DIRECTED

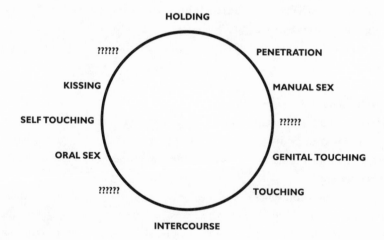

(Illustrations courtesy of Dr. Beverly Whipple.)

As I mentioned above, I have been with my share of men, and when I lost my virginity to one it was a pretty remarkable experience. So I know it's possible to make pleasure instead of PVI (penile-vaginal intercourse) the focal point of sex.

During a recent phone conversation with Whipple about the research about sexuality that she has done throughout her life, I asked her what she would say to women about finding their ultimate orgasm. And the exposed portion of the clit is just the tip. The clit is an impressive organ—the only that's only purpose is pleasure—that is as long as most penises if stretch out fully and looks a little like this. What she said made me tear up.

"You are a very special, unique individual and you have your own areas that feel good to you. You have a right to pleasure, and you have a right to know and respect your body, and you have the right for other people to respect your body. And you have a right to explore your body and find out what feels good to you. And pleasure feels good. If you want to experience your body with someone else, make sure it's consensual and unexploitative, and that it's mutually pleasurable, and that you are honest and free from STIs or protected from them. And that you share your values with your partner."

Amen.

The Basics

Here are the basics when it comes to the science of sex.

When your body realizes that things are about to get good, blood rushes to your vagina and clitoris. At the same time, your vagina starts to lubricate itself.

Your pelvis continues to enjoy increased blood flow as things get more and more interesting. Breathing speeds up. Your nipples may become erect. You may also feel a great deal of tension building up throughout your vulva, vagina, pelvis, backside, and even thighs. It's your muscles and nerves getting ready for what they hope is coming—an orgasm.

(Note: For you science geeks, Masters and Johnson's 1966 work, *Human Sexual Response,* John Bancroft's *Human Sexuality and Its Problems,* and Erick Janssen's *The Psychophysiology of Sex* are all excellent resources for further information about the physical phenomenon of female orgasm.)

When an orgasm does happen, your body experiences contractions wherever the tension was being held, and the feeling, as you hopefully know, is heavenly. The greater the tension, the more delicious and enormous the sensation, which is all about the release of a combination of beta-endorphins (a powerful pain suppressor produced in the pituitary gland), prolactin (best known as the hormone that stimulates milk production after childbirth), and oxytocin (often called the "bonding hormone" because it makes us feel all warm and fuzzy about the person we're with).

Sex is not Tab A into Slot B. It's not PVI. Defining it that way discounts LGBT sex, and any other kind of sex, for that matter, that does not fit into that narrow box.

Sex is mutual pleasure and consent. It's a no-holds-barred sensory exploration and explosion. Sex is consensually doing whatever, however, with whomever, in the pursuit of achieving what you know as your ultimate orgasm.

Knowing what works, being comfortable talking to your partner or partners, experimenting generously—all of those things will lead you to the kind of mind-blowing orgasms that we all deserve. And, yes, good orgasms are an inalienable right. Our forefathers may have forgotten to include that in the Bill of Rights, perhaps because our foremothers were left at home cooking and cleaning and raising the children. But, believe me, they meant to. Or, at the very least, they should have.

This book is about setting out on a journey as a way for you to learn everything you can about female orgasm, so you can find your ultimate orgasm. It might be unsettling at times. It may even be scary. Some things might make you feel angry. And others might make you feel sad. Some things will surprise you and other things will feel like coming home. But one thing is for sure: If you're willing to go along for the ride, it'll all be worth it.

Ultimate orgasm. Every woman has one. And you, my friend, are about to discover yours...

2

Discovering My Ultimate Orgasm

I GREW UP IN a house where *The Joy of Sex* was on the bottom shelf in the family room, but the closest thing I got to a sex talk was a year too late.

I grew up thinking that sex was a thing that boys wanted and girls shouldn't want.

I grew up chasing after boys because I didn't know it was okay for me to chase girls, despite my parents' complete lack of homophobia.

I grew up wondering why on earth people would even do that sex thing.

So some days, it's hard to imagine how I got here. But here I am.

It's impossible to be a woman writing a book about female orgasm and not write about your own experience. And when it comes to orgasm, I consider myself a reasonably fulfilled girl over my lifetime, and an exceptionally satisfied girl these days.

I've had a number of male partners and enough female partners to know the score. I've had some okay partners and I've had some truly impressive partners. But sitting here now looking back over all of my experiences, I am acutely aware of the one thing all of those experiences had in common—me.

The best sex I've had has happened when I am at my best, with a partner who is as interested in my pleasure as in his or her own. When I say "at my best," I don't mean age or body or even general happiness or being in love. I mean *in it*. Really and truly *in it*.

For me, having an otherwise unfathomable orgasm is about being in my body and mind and being invested in that orgasm. Sure, there may be those girls out there who are telling the truth when they say they can come at the drop of a hat, from nothing more than penetration, from a sound or a smell or a thought, no touch required.

For the rest of us regular girls, however, insane orgasms—ultimate orgasms—are very much within our reach, but not, most often, without some serious desire and intent on our parts. My pussy needs to be one hundred percent committed if it's going to happen, and so does my brain. Our brains are wonderful and dangerous things. They can take us on amazing journeys. But they can also keep us from enjoying any of the steps, from first to last, if they so choose.

For me, having my brain in the right place was something I learned from the very beginning of my journey as a sexual person.

"You are responsible for your own orgasm," my very first boyfriend told me the very first time we had sex, when I was seventeen. He wasn't being lazy. He just wanted me to know that I was in control. I was then and I have been ever since. In many ways, I believe that's the key to being orgasmic.

That night, he carried me up to his room, Cyndi Lauper's "Time After Time" playing on the stereo, candles burning in mismatched holders. I came that night, over and over, and I was absolutely mesmerized. I didn't know it then. But I came because I was experiencing blended orgasms, which we will discuss in a number of the chapters coming up.

He fingered me and went down on me and always made sure my clit got the stimulation it needed. He was at least two years my senior and he knew what he was doing. I am eternally grateful for that. He has no idea, but he paved the way for the girl I am sexually today.

That seems like a very, very long time ago now. I have since had my share of partners, men and women alike, and I have had my share of good sex and bad. I've faked my share of orgasms and I have learned my lesson from making that very bad choice. I've been in threesomes and more-somes. I've been tied up and spanked till I was black and blue. I've been burnt with candle wax and had sex in public places.

All of that was fun and exciting and interesting. But none of it taught me about who I was at my core sexually, and none of it brought me to what I have come to know as my own ultimate orgasm. And I'll tell you why: I wasn't focused enough on what I was looking for to know when I found it.

There was a time in my life when sex meant a man snuggling up against my back, spooning me, playing with my clit until I was wet, and then climbing on top of me—or me climbing on top of him. I love the feeling of a partner's weight on me. But I could never come like that.

If I was on top, I had a chance if he could last long enough for me to rub my clit on his pubic bone. Although I have had partners complain that I rubbed them raw and the pain was a serious turn-off. Regardless of whether I came or not, he would come and we would be done for the most part. Some would ask if I wanted him to "finish me off," which always made me feel like my orgasms were an afterthought.

Sure, I had some excellent male partners who ate or fingered my pussy till I came. But I was never in a relationship, even with the most amazing men, where my orgasm was equal to his. The best ones were the one-night stands or occasional repeat partners. But unless it was first-impression sex, the bread-and-butter sex always ended up being like I described above.

You could say I just had a bad run. But I don't buy it. When I had great sex with men, I had to really advocate for myself, and they were often quite surprised. Happy to oblige, but quite surprised.

But when I had sex with women, it was totally different. There was no road map. There were just two people who wanted to get each other off. That was when I learned what my body wanted and needed and what it was capable of.

A study was released in August 2014 that proved what many of us have long known: Lesbians have higher instances of orgasms than straight women when they have sex, something that both Kinsey and Masters and Johnson posited long ago. In other words, a woman engaging in sex with another woman is more likely to have an orgasm then if she was engaged in sex with a man. Women reported experiencing orgasm 62.9 percent of the time. Lesbian women reported an orgasm rate of 74.7 percent (Garcia et al. 2014).

Why? Well, the study offers, "One possible explanation is that self-identified lesbian women are more comfortable and familiar with the female body and thus, on average, are better able to induce orgasm in their female partners. Similarly, previous research has suggested that the length of sexual encounters varies as a function of the sex/gender of the participants, with two women having longer durations of sexual activity than heterosexual pairs [27–29], potentially affecting orgasm outcomes" (Garcia et al. 2014).

The study also suggested that less rigid gender roles, more knowledge of the female body, more variety in sexual activities, and less focus on "performance" led to the increase in orgasms for lesbians over heterosexual women.

It seems funny to me, but it wasn't until now, while writing this book, that I began to experience and understand what exactly my own ultimate orgasm is. It's crazy, I know. But it's true. Researching this book very quickly turned into my own Personal Orgasm Project (P.O.P.).

It's like a lot of things, I guess. I was having okay enough sex. So, I didn't give it much thought. I was just happy to be having it. And then, as I was working on this book, I started asking myself, "Are you having the best possible sex you could be having? Are you trying all the things? Are you as present as you could be? Are you asking for what you want? Are you being honest about what your desires actually are? Are you having sex the way you would if you didn't have any preconceived notions about having sex the way you think you 'should'?"

The answer to all of those questions was the same. "I don't know. But I sure would like to find out."

And at that point it felt like all of the planets aligned, because here I had this project, and I happened to be with a partner, a very new partner, who was game to embark on the project with me. No holds barred. Even when things had the potential to get scary or to feel embarrassing, we kept the space safe for one another and we pushed the boundaries and limits that we then realized were insanely arbitrary. And just like that, we started having the kind of sex we had both always wanted to have.

Okay, maybe it wasn't just like that. There was plenty of trial and error and "oops"es and "oh"s and even more hysterical laughter and confessions and on more than one occasion asking, "Am I a pervert?" But it wasn't long before we let ourselves be ourselves, and although I didn't find my ultimate orgasm with that particular partner, I came much closer than I ever had before.

It was kind of amazing, and I feel very lucky to have experienced that with someone. But I don't think there was anything special about us. Not at all. It's funny. When I wanted to learn to ski, I read up on it and took lessons. Same with rock climbing and sandboarding and scuba diving and rappelling and hang gliding and any number of other adventures I take part in.

And even though I write about sex a lot (and I read an awful lot about it too), I didn't think I needed any lessons or to do any more field work. I figured I was having orgasms. I was a decent masturbator. What more could a girl ask for? The answer is, a lot, actually. Because there is nothing like learning from an expert and focusing your work in the field.

So once she and I started focusing and things started getting really good, I decided it was time to look for a way to up the ante. And I found it.

There's an eighty-five-year-old woman, notorious in feminist and sex-positive circles, who holds naked workshops in her New York City apartment that teach women how to have and enhance their orgasms. Her name is Betty Dodson.

She is the author of the insanely bestselling book *Sex for One* and has been the consummate orgasm and masturbation guru since the '70s. You might call her a founding mother of women's sexual liberation. I certainly would.

I attended one of those famous Bodysex workshops, and even for a girl like me who already felt pretty good about her pussy and her orgasms, it was life-changing.

"Jenny! I was supposed to meet you at the door naked," the gorgeous woman standing before me said before flinging her arms around me. She was almost naked, wearing a thin white tank top that barely covered her behind. "I'm Carlin," she said. Carlin Ross is the business partner of famed sex educator Betty Dodson.

"Come on, let's get undressed," Carlin said, like it was the most normal thing in the world. And if you're there for one of Betty's famous Bodysex workshops, it is. I followed her back to the vestibule at the entryway of Betty's Madison Avenue apartment, and I slipped out of my yoga pants and T-shirt as she slipped out of her tank top.

As Carlin greeted the other attendees coming in, I went into the main room where BackJacks were set up in a circle, each with a towel on it, a pillow behind it, and a tray next to it with a box of Kleenex, a glass of water, a bottle of almond oil, a Dodson Vaginal Barbell, and a Mystic Wand vibrator.

As I tried to decide where to sit, I heard someone say, "Jenny. You're Jenny Block. We know each other." I panicked for a minute. What if she was a PTA mom from my daughter's school? What if we didn't like one another? What if…

"I was at your book signing. In San Francisco. For *Open*. At Good Vibrations," she said.

"Oh!" I said, incredibly relieved. She hugged me, and it took me a minute to remember I didn't have any clothes on. Already it seemed perfectly reasonable to be naked with strangers.

More women filled the room and we all began to take our seats. It's an interesting quandary trying to decide how to sit naked in a room full of strangers. Legs straight out. Like a pretzel. One knee up. Before I could really decide, Betty entered the room.

I was in awe. Eighty-five years old and she walked in as naked as the rest of us and settled into her BackJack as if this scenario was the most common thing in the world, which, to her, it was. Although she has taken a hiatus recently, Betty began doing these workshops in the '70s.

From that moment forward, in some ways, the entire rest of the two days I spent at the workshop were a blur.

Betty welcomed us and began sharing some of her philosophy about sex and orgasms and vulvas (not vaginas) and bodies. (What we see externally is the vulva. The vagina is the internal canal. Period. Betty has been on a lifelong crusade—and rightly so—to get people to use those words properly.)

We started out by going around the circle, talking about how we felt about our bodies and our orgasms, hinting at why each of us was there.

Three of the eight women were getting certified to teach workshops of their own. One was there because of some level of vulvar shame. I was there to gather info for this very book. The others were there simply to learn how to get more out of masturbation and to better understand their own orgasm.

We then moved on to some breathing and an exercise where we slowly entered our nostrils with our oiled pinkies to expand our breathing and take note of how we should respect any opening we enter. Strange exercise. Excellent point.

Soon it was time to retire to the kitchen for fresh strawberries and cookies. Nothing like nudity and orgasm talk to build up an appetite. Despite the sex talk and naked bodies, it was like any other snack break. Almost.

Our group nudity long forgotten, we gathered in the narrow galley-style kitchen and ate and talked like old friends, giggling to ourselves when our bare bottoms touched the counters as we made room for one another.

"Not to worry," Betty told us. The housekeeper was due in on Monday.

Before too long, Betty rang a tiny bell, indicating that it was time for us to circle up again. She spoke about the power of women, the importance of orgasm, and just how vital this work is. Then it was time. Time for genital show-and-tell. No need to read that again. It said exactly what you think it said.

Carlin set pillows against the wall and laid out towels. She brought out a small standing mirror and an ancient desk lamp. As she did, she teased Betty about wanting to get rid of the lamp because it was so old and heated up too much. Betty scowled at her. She'd been using the lamp since the '70s, and getting rid of it was not an option.

"Next, she'll want to put me out to pasture," Betty said forlornly.

Carlin smiled at her and shook her head. "Okay," she said, redirecting. "Betty will go first and I'll go last."

We had all dragged our towels over and were seated or lying in various positions, our faces now just inches away from Betty's pussy. She spread her legs, oiled her fingers, and then spread her outer and then inner lips.

She literally gave us a tour, reminding us sternly once again that what we were seeing from the outside was her vulva, not her vagina, which was the internal canal.

It was perhaps one of the most profound moments of my life. Like so many other moments during the workshop, it felt tribal and ancient, as if we were gathered in the red tent to be gifted with the wisdom of our sister elder. At the same time, I simply could not stop smiling to myself and thinking in my head about how nuts this was, all of us naked and peering between the legs of this famed octogenarian.

Betty continued her guided tour, showing us how one of her inner lips is quite long. As a kid, she thought it was from favoring that side when she masturbated.

"So I started playing more with the other side," she told us.

Betty joked about the prickliness of gray pubic hair, and she apologized to her pussy, promising to groom her as she looked in the mirror and arranged the hair away from the lips, sharing herself as casually as one might share far less intimate body parts.

Then it was our turn. And one by one we sat next to Betty and spread our legs as we looked into the mirror with Betty and admired our pussies. Betty, with a gloved hand, would point out certain features and "style" each of our pussies for a photo, which Carlin took and later emailed to us.

Betty also has a charming habit of naming the "style" of pussy you have, as well as choosing an architectural period for it. And then she helps you name her, unless you already have a name picked out.

I have a doughnut pussy, she told me as I sat with my knees falling open and my pussy lips spread wide. A doughnut because I have full outer lips that outline the inner lips.

"Your design is perfect," she told me. I'm quite sure I blushed. A perfect pussy according to Betty Dodson—*The* Dodson, as Carlin affectionately calls her, and as we began to call her, too.

"A post-modern pussy," she declared. I couldn't help but grin. "And what about a name?" she asked. "Do you have a name for your pussy?"

"I don't," I told her.

"Cream puff," she said.

"Perfect," I agreed.

And somehow, something that seemed so impossible just a moment before was over and The Dodson was off on her next pussy review. I felt happy and safe and, yes, validated and empowered too. I have never really had any issues with my pussy. But having other women look at you, really look at you, is a powerful experience.

After show-and-tell was through, we wrapped up for the day. One of the women asked what plans we had.

"Usually the groups go out for drinks or dinner together," Carlin told us.

The chatter began about where we should go. We agreed on a restaurant around the corner and set out for the evening. There must have been an incredible energy about us. The crowds along the packed New York sidewalks parted like the Red Sea, and when we got to the restaurant, our waiter asked what we were celebrating.

"Our cunt," one of my new friends offered. I kind of loved it. Our collective cunt. Exactly.

The waiter didn't miss a beat. "So, champagne all around," he said with a smile that nearly took over his face.

The next day, we all showed back up at Betty's apartment and whipped our clothes off as if it were the most natural thing in the world. And, honestly, it was.

"Play is the most important thing when you're little," Betty explained. "You don't get enough of it when you're an adult."

Carlin, who Betty affectionately referred to as her "stunt cunt," demonstrated Betty's Rock 'n' Roll method of masturbation while Betty directed and commentated.

"The body knows a lot more than your head," Betty explained. "Trust your body. Our heads are monsters."

After the demonstration and another short exercise, it was time for the main event, what Betty calls "erotic recess."

Even right up to the moment when we reclined in a circle in the center of the room, holding our Mystic Wands to our pussies while Betty directed us, "More pelvis," "Fuck forward," I wasn't sure I could do it. I wasn't sure I could lie back, let my knees fall to the side, and masturbate toe to toe in a circle of women who I had met just twenty-four hours before.

But then it suddenly seemed as impossible to do as it was ridiculous to decline. How could I, when I was literally going to be sitting at the feet of the master?

So I went to my towel and I did it. I followed the steps. I heard the moans. I began to moan myself. I rocked and rolled. I watched the women around me and was energized and, yes, turned on by the faces and the bodies and the incredible energy that was emanating from everyone. And as time passed, I began to hear some of the other women in the room coming.

One of those women was Betty. I found out later that it's quite rare for Betty to come during a workshop, and she told us it had been two weeks since she had masturbated. So I was thrilled that I could be part of the group that inspired her.

I staved off each orgasm that I felt coming up on me until my brain started to interrupt. Was I having performance anxiety? Was the girl writing a book about orgasm unable to have one in this supercharged setting? Had I missed my orgasm window? Had *la petite mort* (as the French so gracefully refer to orgasm) evaded me?

I raised my hand when I saw Betty stand up, as I had been told to do if I needed help. I figured she would hand me the high-powered Magic Wand (as opposed to the lower powered Mystic Wands we were using) and that would do the trick. But instead, Betty Dodson, The Dodson, fucked me to orgasm.

She sat next to me, put her hand on my chest, and began to move the Vaginal Barbell in and out of my pussy. Instantly the sensations switched. She instructed me to keep rocking my pelvis, to keep breathing, to go with it.

She put her fist against my perineum. She looked right at me. She smiled and encouraged me, and the tears began to fall as they sometimes do right before, during, or after an incredible orgasm. She stopped me from overarching my back, as I am prone to do, and blocking the power of my orgasm.

And then it happened. I began to come and come and come.

Betty stayed with me the whole time, and I collapsed after I'm not sure how many small orgasms and then one grand finale to end all finales.

"Thank you," I managed to squeak out.

"Good girl," she said, patting my chest.

I felt powerful and grateful and even a little blessed. I felt as if the greatest gift had just been given to me without the smallest breath of apology or shame.

Betty went on to help one of the other women, and I rode the after-shocks and slowly reentered reality.

I wandered over to a friend's mat afterward, and we started talking about the erotic recess experience. She had been having a bit of a rough day. She had told us at the start of the workshop that day that she had gotten her period and was feeling headachey and sleepy and all around lousy. So during the erotic recess, she wasn't having much luck in the orgasm department.

She knew I was working on this book, so when we started talking about what makes her come, I mentioned that I was curious about doing a little hands-on research. She said she was quite sure couldn't come, but she was more than game to be my guinea pig.

Feeling incredibly grateful at her generous offer, I knelt between her knees. I started by massaging her thighs. Then I did a slow, focused vulvar massage. I asked if I could enter her, and for a little while we talked while I moved my fingers in and out of her pussy, discussing what felt good and what spot was what and all of that.

She reiterated that she didn't think she could come with all of the commotion in the room and the way she was feeling, and I sensed that she felt a little pressured. I assured her that there was no pressure at all and that we had all the time in the world. And although I didn't have any stake in her coming, I did think an orgasm might have helped how she was feeling. So after our anatomical exploration, I suggested that we pretend we were in our own little bubble and that she focus on herself and her breath and what she was feeling and see where it took us.

Sure enough, after just a few minutes, she had a glorious orgasm, and for the first time all day she felt like herself. It felt like a healing, like I had ministered to a friend, and I felt really lucky to be connected to someone who could allow herself such pleasure with a veritable stranger for no reason other than curiosity about what her body might be capable of with the touch and the right connection to another person. We hugged, and I was blown away at the power of the female mind and the female orgasm and our ability to change our physical state when we forget about the "shoulds" of convention and instead think of nothing else but the way our bodies feel.

It was a profound experience that I won't soon forget.

Several months after the workshop, I asked Amy (not her real name) what the experience was like for her. This is what she had to say:

> I remember the intention of our exploration having nothing to do with coming, but rather investigating the G-spot. As your hands rested on my knees, I could feel that you were fully present with me and that I was safe in your hands. The first part of our session together was spent less on building pleasure and more on exploring my body and your touch. Feedback was constant on both sides, which was fascinating.
>
> I remember you mentioning feeling the urethral sponge expanding with your continued touch—noting how the texture changed. Gradually you ended up with four fingers inside of me, engaged in a slow, rhythmic, "come hither" motion. I remember my body opened up very quickly. It was at this point you suggested I grab the vibrator. Shortly after, I had a wonderful orgasm.

What made this situation so beautifully memorable and transformative was the ability to receive sexual pleasure with a non-sexual intention. From my point of view, it was only really about coming when you suggested grabbing the vibrator and both of us consented to allow it to go there.

Feeling safe to openly explore our bodies not only alone, but with others, will bring us deeper into our sexuality and help us to achieve greater levels of pleasure.

The workshop ended with us splitting into two groups and performing a group massage on each participant. Once again, the vibe was ancient and tribal and healing, as the whole workshop had been.

I felt imbued with an energy that my body recognized as something for which it was desperately hungry. A sexual energy that could change the world if harnessed. I felt so lucky to have had this incredible experience with these truly incredible women.

There's so much more that happened, that changed in me, that changed in all of us. So many funny moments, eye-opening moments, even some sad moments. So many connections. It was fun and silly and serious and life-affirming.

I went to the workshop because I was researching orgasm for my book. I left the workshop knowing so much more about myself and these women and sexuality than I could have imagined.

And, yes, I had one hell of a chain of orgasms. Betty Dodson may be eighty-five. But she's right. She's got skills. "Give me any woman, any age, and I'll get 'em off," Betty told us when the workshop began. Indeed.

But the journey did not stop there. That night, I had the pleasure of spending a few private hours with one of my classmates. She knew I was writing this book, and she had seen me bring Amy to orgasm during the workshop and was curious about what it might be like to be with a woman. I was happy to oblige. I feel grateful to women who are game to play and explore in search of their ultimate orgasm, leaving behind any expectations or preconceived notions in terms of how they have defined sex for themselves up until that moment.

We played for hours. The focus was all on her, something we both wanted. And the evening ended in her having what looked to be a gorgeously full orgasm. Several weeks later, I asked her what the experience was like for her, to have the clock become irrelevant and to have a partner interested in nothing more than her pleasure. She teased me that I had ruined her.

"It raised my expectations of how good it could feel," she said. And she found herself marveling at what "the process to orgasm" can look like. "The tension wasn't there because you knew what you were doing and you were dedicated and you enjoyed it.

"I really appreciated the presence and care and focus. It raised my expectations of how a partner could treat me, and I haven't felt that from a man. It taught me a lot about what's possible. It also taught me how much more care and time I could take with myself, because I definitely rush my own masturbation."

It was a bit of a "science experiment" for us both, and it was a powerful reminder to me that that really is the only way to find your ultimate orgasm: with someone who has no ulterior motives, nothing but time and a willingness to give you the space to explore.

I feel incredibly lucky to have experienced that and to be exploring it with yet another partner now as I write this—with the person with whom I did discover my ultimate orgasm, in fact. I would challenge you to settle for nothing less in your own life.

It's funny, really. We share pleasure when we eat good food or scale a mountain or dip into a natural hot springs under a clear blue sky. We cry at plays and gasp at films together. We share all sorts of emotional experiences. But when it comes to sexual pleasure, we don't even share our experiences verbally, let alone actually witness one another sexually.

But everyone wants and needs validation that they're normal. And that's close to impossible to come by if we keep so much about our sexual selves to ourselves. All we know of human sexuality, in many ways, is fake, photoshopped porn images, hiding anything of our real selves from view. It's a shame. Because if we saw the real thing, we wouldn't be so bowled over by the media versions. We need to talk more about sex.

What it's like for us. What we're looking for. We need to ask questions and trust and rely on each other instead of on Google for reassurance and information.

We have to talk about how women's sexuality is different from men's. We have to talk about sexual history and how women used to be treated for "hysteria" by being masturbated to orgasm by their doctor. (That's how the vibrator was invented, in fact. Women weren't crazy. They needed to have some healthy orgasms. Check out *Sex at Dawn* for a great history and explanation of that amazing phenomenon.) We have to talk about how research fails us as women when it comes to orgasm and how our own experiences trump the lab.

You can start by talking to your friends—to anyone you trust, actually. And you need to talk to your partner. If that's someone brand new, it's all the easier because you can start out fresh.

There is a wonderful power to being sexually involved with someone new. You can be the person you have always wanted to be, and there's no one to question you. So if you have the luxury of taking on a new partner, think about who you want to be sexually. What would your authentic self look like? It might be a little uncomfortable at first, as you'll be trying on a new you. But it can be incredibly rewarding to take the leap and exercise your whole self instead of hiding it out of fear of rejection.

When I met one of my past partners, I was really nervous about what the sex would be like. In my mind, she was a "real" lesbian and I was just a "baby" one, despite having been in a relationship with a woman for eight years and having been with a number of women. The truth was that most of the women I had been with had identified as straight before they met me. I had only briefly hooked up with a woman who identified as a lesbian. And here was this woman, who was sixteen years old when she came out, who had been with a number of women before we met. I was afraid she might eat me alive—not in a good way—and laugh at me. Instead, she was actually quite shy and demure. The woman she had been with just before we got together had been married to a man prior to dating her and was incredibly uncomfortable with sex and her own body. When we hit the sheets, she deferred to me. She may have presented as soft butch to the world. But she was as femme as they come in bed. So I decided this was my big chance. I could be whoever I wanted to be sexually, whoever I had always imagined myself to be but was never quite able to manifest. If she didn't like it, well, nothing ventured, nothing gained. But if she did, I could finally be my actual, whole self.

And I'll be damned. Not only did it work, she said that my doing it allowed her to do exactly the same. So what were those things I did, exactly? Well, they weren't earth-shattering, I can tell you that. They were really quite simple:

1. Being present.
2. Asking for what I wanted.
3. Keeping my eyes open during sex and orgasm.
4. Really looking at her body and at her pussy. (And telling her how much I was turned on by her looking at me.)

That's it. That's who I am sexually. Present, observant, and self-advocating. Like I said, not rocket science. Really, those are the fundamentals of what I hope we can all be sexually. The rest, the particulars, that's just window dressing. If you have these basics, you really do have it all.

So, if I'm with someone new, I start from the top. I start with what's real and true, and then I never have to untangle and get out from whatever sexual lies I've woven. That's why faking is so damn dangerous. Once you fake, you've said, "I like what you're doing." So to then have to retreat from that can make your partner feel very untrusting and very unsafe.

Lesson learned. If I'm with someone that I'd like to stay with, but I want to improve my orgasmic life, I know it's time for some serious truth-telling. And you know what? It's never easy and it's never comfortable and it rarely feels good. But how often does change feel good right at the get-go? How often does learning something new feel comfortable during the first lesson? Almost never. But how many times has the result been worth the discomfort? 99 percent of the time, in my experience, whether it's been moving or breaking up or changing jobs or learning to scuba dive.

My orgasm is important enough to tell the truth about and to do the work to get to where I want to be, which is exactly where I am now: having the most incredible sex of my life, adventurous, open, loving, exploratory, and real.

At the time of this writing, I'm exploring with a new partner, my girlfriend Lacey, someone with whom I am deeply in love and who is young and confident and open. She is androgynous in appearance, with short hair and a distinct preference for gorgeous custom-tailored suits and a leather jacket that makes me weak in the knees.

I find my attraction to her curious and surprising, as "girly girls" were long more my thing. That might explain the intense attraction and stellar sex I'm now experiencing. If you've always been even slightly mismatched, finding your match—not to mention being deeply in love—makes for the kind of sex that you think is only myth.

She teased me mercilessly for a week before we ultimately had sex. It was shockingly good. Not "good for the first time" sex. But actually good. Really good, in fact. And over the months that followed, things have only gotten better.

And I can tell you exactly why.

One, the match, yes. We are very good together. And two, yes, we both enjoy and have an aptitude for sex.

But most importantly, we talk about sex—before, during, and after. We ask for what we want. We talk dirty. We "debrief." It may sound silly, and you may think so much talking would ruin things. But nothing could be further from the truth. The sex is great because we decided it was going to be and because we are committed to one another's pleasure. It's as simple—and perhaps as complicated—as that.

It's the first time in a long time that I have ventured into monogamy, which I think has upped the ante for us both.

All I know is that it's working. And it's the kind of sexual adventure—and love—I wish for anyone who is interested in pleasure and discovery first and rules never. We have created a safe space for one another all around, and that is key when it comes to discovering your ultimate orgasm.

I'm not suggesting that it's easy to be in this place. Not at all. It's quite hard in some ways, because it's about being vulnerable and transparent and open to risk, and you have to feel safe and respected in order to be able to do that. It took me a long time to get there. But now that I'm here, the orgasms I'm being rewarded with are well worth what it took to get to this place. I have finally found my ultimate orgasm.

3

Behind the Curtains

OKAY. SO I KNOW what you're thinking. All of that philosophy and personal history of mine is all well and good. But I know that's not what you came here for. You came for the good stuff, the stuff that's going to get you to *your* ultimate orgasm, and I'm not going to make you wait for it. Before we even get into the how-to's and the mysteries and all of that, let's get down to the nitty-gritty.

This book will give you a heck of a lot more info as you go. But as I did my research, I was amazed by the things that topped the list of concerns and came up over and over again in my research, my survey, and my casual conversations with friends, strangers, and colleagues—of which there have been many—while writing this book.

So, if you're like me and are in the habit of reading the last chapter of a book first because you simply can't wait to get to the good part, I thought I would make it easy for you. In some ways, I'm starting at the end, with the topological map of orgasm, as my little sister, ever the researcher, called it. The big-picture overview of the top concerns women raise when it comes to orgasm.

We're all looking for the ultimate orgasm, and this book will lead you to finding yours. In the meantime, here are some high-level orgasm principles to whet your appetite, quell your curiosity, and prepare you for the deluge of delicious orgasm information that is to come.

There's no shame in getting started.

Where do you start on your path to ultimate orgasm if having orgasms is not even a regular occurrence for you? Well, I say, fake it till you make it.

I would never suggest you actually fake it. That sends the wrong message to your partner. But getting in the zone by mimicking the things your body does when you are aroused can really get things going. Here are some easy ways to do that while engaging in sexual play:

1. Use lube. As soon as you feel that slipperiness between your legs, your body will get the hint to get wetter.
2. Control your breathing. Start paying attention as you inhale and exhale, and speed up to bring your body up to speed.
3. Make some noise. There's nothing like a little moaning and a few well-meaning ooohs and ahhhs to signal to your body what's to come.
4. Get moving. Moving your pelvis is a great way to tell your body that things are about to get interesting. So don't be shy about lifting your hips or wiggling your backside. And believe me, your partner won't be complaining about the pre-show.
5. Talk dirty. There is nothing like saying words, all the naughty, otherwise "unsayable" words like pussy and wet and cock and fuck, to get your body and mind (and your partner's body and mind) really and truly into it.

All of these things can help to rev you and your partner up, which means you'll get even more of that sexual attention you're craving. It's a win-win-win.

Fingers are the ultimate instruments of pleasure for women.

The penis is what brings a man pleasure. But that does not mean that it is the primary instrument for bringing a woman pleasure. More on that in Chapter Seven. For now, it is imperative for you to know that a person's fingers can more likely bring you to orgasm than any penis or other phallus can.

"Many a woman swears that, hands down, nothing gets her off to a flying start and then accomplishes the mission like a lover's adept fingers" (Schell 2011, 75). We all think it. It's time we all said it. We like fingers, and for us, that's not foreplay. It is *the* play.

Knowing this can allow you to advocate for what you desire. It's okay to say that you prefer your partner's fingers over all else. It's not a dis or a commentary on a man's manhood. It is just a fact, and it's imperative that your partner understand that and not take it personally.

It is vital for you both to understand that although you may be happy to have a man penetrate you for his pleasure, and although you may derive some pleasure from it, you are ultimately doing it for him. Not for you. There's not a thing in the world wrong with that if it gives you pleasure to allow him to find his pleasure inside you. And women have all sorts of delicious nerve endings inside their pussies, so it makes perfectly good sense that being penetrated would feel good to us. But you do not owe it to a man to sacrifice your pleasure for his ego.

This is generally not an issue in a lesbian relationship because fingers are already presumed to be central during sex. But heterosexual women should take a page from the lesbian sex playbook on this one. Being a lesbian is not what makes fingers so satisfying. Being a woman is. Just because you might be straight shouldn't mean you have to settle for a less satisfying sex life. It just means that you will likely have to lay out that sex, for you, means mutual pleasure, and that your instrument of choice for your ultimate orgasm is fingers (likely as part of what I mentioned early on—the magical blended or combo orgasm).

LET YOUR FINGERS DO THE WALKING...

Your fingers are extremely communicative. You can feel and transmit very subtle sensations with your fingers. Your fingers are also dexterous. They can bend and reach to explore every nook and cranny. You can use your fingers as a prelude to something, well, bigger—more fingers, a hand, or a dildo—or as the main attraction. Not everyone wants four fingers inside her vagina, and those who do may enjoy the feeling of slowly adding fingers one at a time.

You can caress the opening of the vagina, and your partner can squeeze your fingers as you find her most sensitive spots. You can easily reach her G-spot by angling your fingers towards the front wall of the vagina. Try caressing her G-spot with varying pressure and speed, as you would the glans and hood of her clit.

As the receptive partner, you can push out toward your partner's hand; your G-spot will be apparent as an area of tissue that's spongier and rougher than the rest of your vagina.

You can use one hand for penetration, reserving the other for clitoral stimulation. The finger circling her clit can match the rhythms of the finger thrusting inside her. You can hold the vibrator to her clit, or she can touch herself—leaving you to concentrate on her vagina. With two or three fingers you can rapidly thrust in and out, pumping at a pitch that you couldn't possibly sustain with a strap-on dildo. (Newman 1999, 187–189)

You can make it last as long as you like.

Many women ask me how they can make their orgasm last longer. This can be tricky, but it's well worth it once you master the technique. When you feel as if you are about to come, slow down or back up or do whatever it takes to ease off without stopping completely.

Then, build back up to where you were and do that again and again until you can't take it anymore. It's possible that it will feel as if you have backed off too much and now you can't have an orgasm at all.

In that case, take a break. If you're playing with a partner, massage your partner, make out with your partner, or start teasing your partner in his or her favorite ways. Then get back to yourself later. If you're playing alone, get your mind in the zone. Read some erotica. Watch some sex-positive, woman-positive porn. Massage your thighs and breasts. But give your pussy a break for a bit. Then get back to business when you think you're ready.

Lacey is a master at this, at reading my body language and keeping me right on the razor's edge. Sex lasts for hours and the pleasure is prolonged and spreads through my whole body. Interestingly, it can lead to some of the most insanely intense and explosive orgasms, as well as the most delicious and sublime and delicate and prolonged ones, because my body comes so close so many times before actually reaching orgasm. I like to call it the Push-Pull method: You push your body as far as you can go, and then you pull back and repeat.

This practice is definitely a learned skill, and I'm still working hard at mastering it. I believe our record to date is a five-minute-long, prolonged orgasm, which is different from the multiples that I am also over the moon to be experiencing these days. So, trust me, it's definitely possible. And it's the most fun you'll ever have practicing something!

There's never a reason to settle.

We have to expect our partners—whether they be men or women—to accept and adore the reality of our bodies and how they work. Other-wise, we have to stop granting them the honor of enjoying our bodies sexually.

It's a lot like buying a car. That car dealer will have you believing that if you don't buy that car right that minute, there will never ever be another one like it and you will never find a deal as great as this one.

But precisely the opposite is true. There are *more* than enough cars and *more* than enough deals. The dealer needs you *way* more than you need him.

So too is it with sexual partners. We don't give ourselves enough credit as women. We settle for the scraps. We take what we can get. We come in a mediocre way once in a while and we call that a success for the privilege of "getting" to be with that person.

That's a bunch of bunk.

There are amazing partners out there, and those are the only ones you have any need to bother with. If a partner thinks that PVI or penetration is the end-all be-all, then you keep on walking. Nothing to see here. No need to have your pleasure relegated to foreplay.

My pleasure is not the prologue or the epilogue. It is the main act that contains the arc of the story. And I will not relegate or sacrifice it.

There are four keys to facilitating an orgasm for a woman who has never had one.

Patience, presence, pathos, and pace. Those are the four keys to helping a woman reach orgasm when she never has before.

Be patient. That's the most important thing. Listen to what her experience has been, what her fears may be, and what her desires are. Ask her questions and be prepared to hear the answers. Ask her if she has any questions. Most—not all, but most—women who have never had an orgasm have trouble getting and staying in their bodies and keeping their head in the game. They may be distracted by past trauma or experiences. Or they may have body issues. Or they may worry about how an orgasm will feel, if they will be able to have one, what they will sound like, and so on. If you want to help a woman reach orgasm, being patient is paramount.

Be present. Every woman's experience is unique when it comes to orgasm. Facilitating one for someone, especially for someone who has never had one, is about being able to meet her where she is and help her to get to where she wants to be. Stay in the moment with her and she will be eternally grateful.

Have pathos. Being understanding of what a woman trying to reach orgasm is going through will make all the difference when it comes to whether or not this will be her breakthrough. Regardless of your own orgasm experience, do your best to put yourself in her place and understand how challenging and perhaps embarrassing or scary this might be.

Be mindful of her pace. Take your time and let her know that she can take her time too. Most women can't and don't come in an instant, especially the first time around and especially if her path to orgasm has been a long and challenging one. Start with sensual activities like a full-body massage, and then work up to breast massage and ultimately vulvar massage. Once she is fully relaxed and aroused, then consider moving on to clitoral stimulation, penetration, oral sex, and the rest. This is the fun part. Don't rush. The longer the tease, the more fulfilling the please.

Women don't take "too long" to come, and facilitating female orgasm is not "hard work."

First of all, orgasm—having one or facilitating one—should never, ever be considered work, unless it is actually your career. Orgasm is one of life's greatest pleasures, and if it's your orgasm and it feels like work, it's time to rethink what orgasm means to you.

And it's time to consider a new partner if it's your partner's orgasm that you don't want to be troubled with. Getting to the orgasm should be at least half the fun for any and all parties involved. If it isn't, consider whether you've taken note of what this book has to offer about the ins and outs of maximizing your orgasm-having and -giving.

The second major issue here is why there is any comparing at all going on. Men's orgasms and women's orgasms are very different. There's no need to compare them and, honestly, no good can come from that. In fact, comparing them, to my mind, is what got us into the orgasm mess we're in now. It doesn't take women "too long." It takes as long as it takes. It doesn't take "too much" to get a woman to come. It's just a delusion that a few strokes of a penis in a vagina is some sort of cause for celebration.

If women are going to have happy, healthy orgasmic lives, we've got to recalibrate. Men's and women's orgasms are equally good and equally important and very much different. Once we all come to accept those truths, issues like this will arise less frequently—and show-stopping orgasms will arise far more frequently.

It may have taken you a long time to have your first one, and that doesn't matter.

I don't know specifically why it took so long for the number of readers who asked this question. I do know that I found it intriguing that they posed the question at all. My guess is that these women feel as if they missed something or that perhaps something was or is wrong with them.

But the truth is, a variety of factors could have contributed to the fact that it was a long time coming for them to start coming. And all that matters now is that they are coming. So, do your best to let it go if this is one of those questions that plagues your own mind. If it's all good now, it's all good!

Orgasm can be so darn elusive sometimes.

Orgasms are fickle fellows. They are as dependent on our bodies as they are on our minds. Depending on the time of month, how much sleep you've had, whether you've been drinking, who you're with, whether or not you're alone, what kind of sex acts you're partaking in, and so on and so on, sometimes an orgasm may be really hard or even impossible to come by.

Even though this whole book is about how important orgasms are and how to have them, it's also about learning not to put so much focus on the orgasm itself. Pleasure should be the focus, not necessarily orgasm. And, like with a lot of things, once you stop chasing it, it will likely come to you with ease.

Why is it hard sometimes? Because it is. Because it's the human body we're talking about here. So set your mind at ease. Think of sex as play. Sometimes the game has a dramatic conclusion and sometimes it's to be continued...

You never have to feel intimidated when it comes to orgasm.

Intimidation is an interesting emotion. I went on a date with a woman once who told me she wasn't sure she would ever want to sleep with me because she was intimidated by me.

"Why?" I asked.

"You're literally writing the book on orgasm," she said, laughing.

It was funny, because *I* felt incredibly intimidated by *her*—because of her work (she's an incredibly successful DA in Los Angeles); because her "time in the field" far outweighs mine when it comes to being with women; and, quite honestly, because she's a butch of the Shane from *The L Word* kind.

I was glad for the conversation, because it made me think about something absolutely vital to this conversation. We should never be intimidated by someone's perceived knowledge about all things sex, because the truth is, it doesn't really matter. It's basically a clean slate every time.

Sure, I've read all the books and tried all the tricks. But as soon as I'm with someone new, it's a whole new game on a whole new playing field.

Killer orgasms are about lifelong learning. Our way of looking at sex morphs and changes and grows. It should, anyway. If you stop exploring, you might as well forget about expanding your orgasmic capacity.

So don't be intimidated by a new partner, or allow a current partner to be intimidated by new interests you may be developing. In so many ways, we are all new. Every sexual experience has the capacity to be new.

Be open to giving and receiving and listening and hearing, and you will be bowled over by the kind of orgasms you will begin to have. So many of our orgasmic limitations have to do with expectations and preconceived notions. The brain gets too busy and the body doesn't have a chance to enjoy.

Case in point: One night I went home with a girl who had kissed another woman before, but had otherwise only been sexual with men. She seemed to be enjoying the play but simply could not reach orgasm. She told me the next day that she just couldn't let go enough to go there despite the fact that she expected to be able to.

Interestingly, in the middle of it all, she offered—unsolicited—that what she didn't expect to be able to do was to go down on a woman. But, out of nowhere, she did, and I had an incredibly intense orgasm. She was tickled that she could go there and enjoy it and was able to make me come, giving her a renewed sexual energy and sense of power, almost as good as having an orgasm herself!

So leave intimidation at the door. If it's at play in any of your sexual endeavors, tell it to hit the road. And if the person causing it won't allow it to leave on its own, he or she is welcome to go with it. There's no room for that in pursuit of the ultimate orgasm.

For many women, the blended orgasm is the ultimate orgasm.

Throughout this book, we're going to talk about all kinds of zones and places from which orgasm can emanate. But it's important that you know, right from the get-go, that for most women, the blended (or combo) orgasm is their definition of the ultimate orgasm.

The idea of the blended orgasm is rooted deeply in science; it is based on the fact that the clitoris has "legs" nestled within the vagina as well as a tip exposed on the outside. So, tending to the clitoris in a variety of ways in a variety of places will lead to the kind of explosive, winding, lengthy, ultimate orgasm for which most of us long.

This means engaging the tip of the clit externally, while also engaging the breasts, anus, skin, brain, G-Zone, and/or A-Zone at the same time using the fingers, toys, the mouth, or other body parts as you see fit.

This book is about not limiting yourself to the current primary definition of sex. Sex is pleasure. No need to limit that.

This isn't just an "add ingredients and stir" situation.

When women ask me about adding "variation" to their sex life, it implies to me that anything other than PVI is out of the norm and thus a "variation." When it comes to sex, everything and nothing is a variation. Everything and nothing is normal. We have to start looking at sex as a buffet. You don't have to pick one main course. You don't even have to pick one from column A and one from column B and one from column C.

What is sex, anyway, really? Oral? Anal? Vaginal? Kissing? Fingering? Fisting? Flogging? Yes, yes, yes, a thousand times yes. It's all of that or, if you prefer, none of that. What it isn't—at least not in its entirety—is the insanely limited act of a man putting his penis inside of a woman's vagina. That is *a* sexual act. It is not *the* sexual act.

So, in answer to those questions about variation: You can do all kinds of things. Start with making sure your clit is getting the attention it wants. Use your fingers or a vibrator, or have your partner tend to it. Add some anal play. Or a little light (or heavy, for that matter) BDSM. Spanking, slapping, biting, whipping—whatever lights your fire. The list is endless. The answer is—anything and everything.

Depending on your partner to "make you come" is a setup for failure.

You can't. You shouldn't. Don't. It isn't fair. To either of you. To quote my very first boyfriend once again, "You are responsible for your own orgasm." No one else can know exactly what you like or exactly how something feels. There is nothing more frustrating than being expected to be a mind reader.

If you like it, say so. If you don't like it, say so. If you want more or less or harder or faster, say so. And remember, your partner only has two hands. You have two more. So use them. If it feels good, go for it. Don't ignore your ass or your breasts or your perineum or your mons pubis or behind your knees, or your ears and throat and thighs for that matter. If it feels good, ask your partner to rub, grab, pinch, stroke, or slap it. Or get to it yourself.

It's your body. It's your orgasm. There is no reason for you not to get in there. Forget the pillow-princess crap. Real women have orgasms. In fact, real women have a right to ultimate orgasms.

There are seven things you must have in order to achieve an ultimate orgasm.

Enthusiastic consent. There really is nothing sexier than consent. To enthusiastically consent to orgasm is to give yourself over completely to someone, without holding anything back. When there is no enthusiastic consent, it can be harder to reach orgasm because you may withhold. So choose your partner consciously and enthusiastically.

Relaxation. If you are tense, it can be a challenge to reach orgasm. So whatever you do to relax, add it to your orgasmic practice. A warm shower, a hot bath, some great music, no clock in sight, the lights dimmed. Whatever works for you. Orgasm is a fully sensory experience, so be sure your senses are ready for the ride.

Presence. Allow yourself to totally fall. In love. In lust. *In*. Period. Be where you are in that moment. Forget the laundry and your thighs and whether or not that person is going to call you tomorrow. If you want to have an orgasm, particularly a stellar one, you have to dial in and not phone it in.

Readiness. Come ready to come. Women often find themselves coming to orgasm from a place of scarcity. Not enough time. Not enough head-space. Not enough energy. But the best orgasms come from a place of abundance. So think *ready*. Think *open*. Think *more*. Think *I deserve this*. And be ready to ride every juicy wave that the day's orgasm has to offer.

Quiet. Shut off your mind to the world and tune it in to what you're feeling. For some, a quiet mind requires other kinds of sound—music or white noise or the hum of the city outside. Whatever you need to quiet your mind, do it. There are no wrong answers here.

Attention. Pay attention to every sensation. Every inch of your body reacts differently to touch. And there are so many different kinds of touch. Pay attention to what you're feeling, where you are feeling it, and when you are feeling it. That kind of consciousness will help you to hone in on what works for you and what will lead you to ultimate orgasm.

Breath. I cannot stress enough how important breath is to orgasm. Regulating your breathing before, during, and after sex allows you to be in your body the way nothing else can. Being conscious of your breath is a great way to focus on your body and what it is experiencing, allowing you to stay in the moment and reach orgasm. Holding your breath may cause you not to experience orgasm as fully and deeply as you otherwise would. So pay attention to your breathing and don't allow it to stop or become too shallow. Stay with it—your breath, that is, and your orgasm.

Sex that ends in ultimate orgasms is circular.

Sex starts and ends with kissing and holding and rubbing and rocking and laughing and playing and penetrating and licking and sucking and biting and, well, you get the idea. It's where two people have nothing on their minds but giving and receiving pleasure. It's an endless menu from which both partners can pick and choose, and every time is different.

Orgasms feel different to every woman.

When I asked the women I surveyed how an orgasm feels to them, there was a lot of overlap in their responses. Many women described it as release of some variety—deep release, total release, physical release, release of stress, release of energy, ripple release, release of tension, release of beautiful emotions, even a release akin to the one a sneeze provides ("Like a good sneeze, only a thousand times better and it starts in my pants.")

Many of them also used the word *wave*, referring to waves of intensity or pleasure or ecstasy. And there was a plethora of gloriously active descriptions, with many of the women using words like *throbbing, pulsing, contracting, spasming, exhausting, falling, rushing, exhilarating, satisfying, floating, relaxing, tensing, tingly, pulsating, euphoric, a rush, tightening, liberating, gratifying, freeing, buzzing, exalting, exhausting, exploding, transporting, harrowing, exhausting, all consuming, giggly,* and *high.*

Others described orgasm as feeling tingly, shuddery, like relief, heat, pressure, lightning, a surge of energy, rejuvenation, tension, excited shivering, exaltation, happy electricity, body bliss, total focus, a pinpoint of light that explodes, total focus, letting go, losing control, jumping off a cliff, nerve cells firing, a whole body rush, climbing a mountain then flying off the top and hang gliding back down, ripping out of shedding skin, and a rollercoaster ratcheting up until you reach the top and free-fall to the bottom.

Some talked about it affecting specific body parts, and not just the usual sexual subjects, saying it caused uncontrollable muscle spasms or contractions or crying, while others described it as a true whole-body experience or even an out-of-body experience.

And then there were all of the similes:

Like I'm in outer space.
Like energy shooting out of my toes and fingers.
Like an earthquake inside of me.
Like God, like being God.
Like I'm connecting to my soul battery.
Like being lost and finding myself.
Like my muscles can't support their own weight.
Like a buzzy vibratory separation of spirit and body.
Like my whole body disappears and my ego ceases to be—I turn into something that is not human, or essentially human.
Like searching and then finding exactly what I was looking for.
Like I couldn't be still if I tried.
Like I want to scream. (In a good way!)
Like I just won something.
Like an intense head rush that causes every nerve in my body to become alive.
Like everything in the world is perfect and I have no fucks to give about anyone outside of myself for just a few moments.

Like walking into Disney World for the first time! Completely over-whelming. My entire body feels pleasure. Every sense is initially heightened, then clamps down when I'm coming. I don't see, hear, smell…all I do is live in that moment and exist only for that pleasure.

There were the philosophical responses, too:

Sometimes a starburst, sometimes a falling away.

All of my nerves collect at my groin and sing a song of praise.

A complete release of all that is wrong in my life.

An intense tug and a release on reality.

It reminds me of that moment when you are really into someone but aren't sure they feel the same, that moment of nerves before you kiss for the first time, and then that intense feeling of happiness when you connect.

It feels like something blooming on me…with colors. Opening up and spreading.

They are the most intense pleasure I've ever experienced, and for me there's nothing more empowering than bringing women completely over the edge.

There were a few funny ones too:

If I think about the best feelings I've ever had and stick them in a blender with heat and lack of control. Yay!

Like my vagina just finished a hike to the top of a mountain and then my whole body is happy.

And there were the physiological ones:

I see fireworks like spots behind my eyes.

It takes my breath away, literally.

I have blacked out from a great orgasm.

I see colors and visions.
I can't talk.
I collapse.

And perhaps my personal favorite: *I melt.*

Penetration is not—I repeat, not—the main act.

I realize this is an incredibly political thing to say. But orgasm is political. It's true. We have to let go of the fact that seeking our pleasure may unseat those who have long been in power, and instead focus on the fact that our pleasure is important enough to demand this kind of unseating.

I know. I know. You're a woman and you have had an orgasm from PVI, or you're a man and you are one hundred percent sure that you have made a woman orgasm via PVI. But if that's the case, you are an anomaly, or the planets were aligned just right, or the clit was being stimulated via vibration from intercourse or otherwise. The latter being the most likely explanation.

But whatever the reason, whatever the way, the reality is still the same—penetration alone is not what makes the overwhelming majority of women orgasm, and therefore penetration should not be the center of the sexual universe.

This is good news. Trust me. The pressure is off and the game is on. Men don't have to read a million articles on the "Ten Best Positions to Make Your Woman Come," and women don't have to read anything more about how to forgive themselves for not being multiorgasmic during sex.

If penetration were the central sex act, lesbian sex would focus on it just like heterosexual sex does. Guess what? It doesn't. At all. Penetration is an ingredient. The only main course is pleasure. Want more proof that penetration is more about the man? Take a look at gay male sex. You guessed it: Penetration is the primary sex act because that's what feels good to men.

Penetration is ancillary for sex for women. Period.

There's nothing wrong with intercourse or penetration. It can add a welcome element. But focusing on it as the main event makes it seem as if there is something wrong with women who cannot orgasm from penetration alone. Women are not designed to orgasm from penetration alone. And although not all orgasms are equal—some leave me feeling like I shouldn't drive a motor vehicle or like I'm drifting in outer space—where an orgasm originates or how it comes to fruition simply does not matter. That you are deriving pleasure from the act is the only thing that's important. There is no hierarchy to how you get there. None. If your partner makes you feel like there is, then it's time for a big talk or a new partner. It's as simple as that.

You know, it's amazing. Really health-conscious women do everything in the world for their bodies except tend to their orgasms. They eat right and exercise. But we need orgasms as much as we need good food and good exercise. Women need to have sex. Women need to feel pleasure. Women need to have orgasms. We need to get out of our heads and into our bodies. Because to get into your body is to get into your power.

Of course, many men are going to think that intercourse is sex. That's what they've learned. That's what we've all learned. But we have to reteach. We have to retrain ourselves and each other.

Heterosexual sex should look more like lesbian sex: less linear and more circular. The endgame of sex is not male orgasm. The point and focus of sex is not intercourse. The endgame of sex is pleasure for all involved. The point and focus of sex is to experience pleasure and ultimate orgasms. Although as long as you have the former, you only *have* to have the latter if you so desire.

Sex is about pleasure and touch and connection. It's about wanting to give each other pleasure and getting pleasure from that process. It's not about, "What do I have to do in order to get what I want?" Instead it should be about, "Look at this incredible body that I have the honor and the pleasure of being allowed to enjoy."

You're missing all the fun—all the juicy, inventive, exciting fun—if all you're doing is being a vessel. You have to get in there. You have to lose yourself and give in. You have to be where you are. You have to explore and chase and play. And you have to have a partner who wants to do exactly that for and with you.

I had a male lover for about a year who had trouble getting hard. It was one of the most unique and wonderful blessings in disguise. The focus of sex automatically shifted away from intercourse and toward pleasure of a zillion different varieties. We had the most intense, incredible sessions because we made it up as we went along instead of following the script that was long ago prescribed for making babies, and thus does not necessarily work for facilitating ultimate orgasms for women.

As women, we have to lay down the law and refuse to simply be vessels for anyone else's pleasure. Our vaginas do not exist for the pleasure of others. They are not owed to anyone. When we have a partner, we *share* ourselves, which means giving *and* taking.

It's time to retire the word *foreplay*. The word literally means "playing before," which readily implies that what comes after is the serious, central, main event. It's time we called bullshit on that. It's all sex play. It's all sex. It's all the main event.

As someone who has identified as straight and as bi and now as lesbian, to my mind, lesbian sex is an excellent model for sexual activity. Lesbian sex is built around the premise that both partners should be pleasured and should come, and that neither one's orgasm is more important than the other's and neither one's orgasm marks the end of the event.

Again, I'm not saying all lesbians believe this about sex and I'm not saying all heterosexuals believe that intercourse is the main event and that once he comes, the party is over. But you're kidding yourself if you don't see that the latter is universally held by far too many as truth.

Think of every sex joke and movie sex scene and every story that every best friend has ever told you. You can be angry and defensive about this, or you can accept that this is how it is but shouldn't be, and shift your thinking. As my dad always asks, "Do you want to be happy or right?"

In this case, even if you are sure you're right, you'd be wrong if you think that most people don't hold and haven't held this belief for generations and that it's making orgasms for women a very tough issue.

When someone says *sex*, they most likely mean PVI, the end of which is denoted by male orgasm. When most men come, they are spent and ready for sleep. On the other hand, "After an orgasm, a woman may be anticipating a dozen more. A female body in motion tends to stay in motion. But men come and go. For them, the curtain falls quickly and the mind turns to unrelated matters," as authors Christopher Ryan and Cacilda Jethá (2010, 245) explain in *Sex at Dawn*, their impressive and exhaustive history of sex.

"Even today, women's sex information and education is based on the male model of sexual response: A penis ejaculating inside a vagina. This is also the heterocentric, procreative model that's supported by organized religions, governments, and even Mother Nature who wants to further the species. Some days it seems that women can't win for losing," Dodson (2014) explains in a recent blog post on her site. (This is an excellent piece, by the way—well worth reading!)

And according to a study done at the Kinsey Institute at Indiana University, "95 percent of respondents would consider penile-vaginal intercourse (PVI) having had sex (Sanders 2010).

This is a problem. A big problem, in fact. Why?

1. It makes women think their orgasms are less important than men's.
2. It makes women think they "take too long."
3. It makes women think they should come from PVI.
4. It makes women think they are greedy to want what their bodies are hungering for.
5. It makes women think there is something wrong with them.
6. It makes women embarrassed and ashamed.
7. It makes men think they have a right to spend a few minutes "warming up" a woman before entering her, coming, and calling it a night.
8. It makes men feel inadequate when women don't come from the "warm up and hit it" sex plan.
9. It makes men look at women as sexual second-class citizens.

10. It means men have a more difficult time understanding women's wants, needs, desires, and bodies.

There you have it. The backbone, the basics, the fundamentals of female orgasm. And now, let's dive in.

The Myths and Truths
of Female Orgasm

THERE'S A LOT OF BAD information spinning around out there, and there's a lot of male-centered information. Women orgasm differently from men, and in some ways the act of sex as we currently know and accept it is in opposition to women's pleasure. So let's start by dispelling some myths about female orgasm.

Myths are always dangerous. A myth is not just misinformation, but misinformation that has been perpetuated and glorified and trusted and passed on such that people have begun to accept it as truth.

Whether they are about a point in history, a group of people, or a certain place or activity, myths leave people confused and disappointed. They also cause people to miss out on things because of the misunderstandings that the myths cause.

This could not be any more true when it comes to female orgasm. There are so many myths swirling around, it's a miracle that any of us are having orgasms at all, let alone good ones.

So let's get to debunking the most common ones.

The Myths About Female Orgasm

Myth #1. Orgasm is the only goal when it comes to having sex.

Sex is about pleasure. Sometimes, it's also about connection. Orgasm is a lovely byproduct. But too many people think of sex—and masturbation for that matter—as akin to a road trip. You have a destination and a map and a single tool, your car, to get you there.

Sex should be geared toward exploration rather than destination. There is no map. Even if you've done it a thousand times before, even if you've read it all, done it all, seen it all, each occasion has the opportunity to be a new adventure. So follow it where it leads and keep at it for as long as the pleasure lasts.

Take advantage of all the tools at your disposal. Your body, your partner's body, tongues, hands, feet, fingers—you get the idea. And don't discount toys. There's no reward for having sex without toys. Using them does not mark you as any less competent. Again, the goal is pleasure—as long as it's consensual (and legal), do it.

Satisfaction should be the one and only endpoint. If you have an orgasm, great. If not, don't punish yourself or stress out about it. The only effect that will have is to make it even harder on you the next time.

Relax. This is sex. Not rocket science. Remember: Pleasure, and being satisfied with the level of pleasure you personally reach at that specific moment in time, is the only goal. The only goal.

Myth #2. All women can easily have multiple orgasms.

Women are a lucky bunch. We have the capacity for multiple orgasms. But don't let the movies fool you. That doesn't mean that all women, or even most women, actually have them. And even for those who do, it doesn't mean that it's easy or that it happens each and every time they have sex or masturbate.

This is another one of those times when comparing yourself to other women can be particularly dangerous. If you're worried about having multiple orgasms, how are you even supposed to manage one? There should only be one thing on your mind when you're having sex—pleasure.

"This feels good." That should be what occupies every part of your body and mind during sex. If it isn't, then it's time to readjust. That means either changing the tape that's going through your head or changing what is happening with your body. Either way, having an orgasm is like a lot of things: If you stop worrying about it, you'll have one—or maybe even multiples!

Myth #3. All women like the kind of sex you see in those romantic movies.

Nice girls want to be fucked too. Although porn is dangerous because it implies that women easily come instantly and multiple times and that sex with a man is all about the man, romantic films are equally dangerous because they suggest that all we want is to have our hair gently stroked and our backs rubbed. Fuck that. We want to be fucked too.

All different types of women like to have sex in all different kinds of ways, and desires change all the time. Every time we have sex, in fact. It all depends on so many factors. Whether we are alone or partnered. Who that partner is. Where we're having sex. What kind of day or week we've had. What time of the month it is. In other words, we want what we want, when we want it.

So don't berate yourself if you get nothing out of all that nicey-nicey, touchy-feely stuff and want your partner to really get to it. But keep in mind that even the very best partners aren't mind readers. Although all of the very best partners do want to pleasure you. So tell your partner what you want, how you want it, and when you want it. If you get judged for it, show that partner the door. There's no excuse for sexual shaming. Ever.

Myth #4. It's perfectly fine to fake an orgasm.

Although I can tell you from firsthand experience that no partner I've had has ever known I was faking it, that's nothing to be proud of. I was doing myself a major disservice every time I faked the Big O.

Why? Because I was basically telling my partner that what we did resulted in an orgasm, which implies that said acts bear repeating when— most often—nothing could be further from the truth.

This is one of the many reasons why we have to take the focus off the orgasm as the end-all, be-all, must-do. Sex doesn't always lead to orgasm. But it must always lead to pleasure. So tell the truth every time.

That's not always easy, I know. Especially when you have an eager beaver on your hands who is determined to make you come at all costs. You have to remind your partner that you get to decide what you want done to you and when and for how long, and if you're done, you're done, regardless of whether or not you've had an orgasm.

Myth #5. Having safer sex ruins sex.

That's just crazy talk. Safer sex is actually sexier sex because one, it shows that your partner cares about you enough to protect you, and two, it allows your brain not to worry about pregnancy or STIs and instead to focus on the important thing at hand—playing with your partner!

One of the times I felt most cherished by a partner was when she got up to wash her hands after having had her finger in my backside. She apologized when she excused herself to wash up, and I said, "Never apologize for taking such good care of me."

(Note: This may be obvious, but it bears mentioning. Never put anything in your vagina or even on your vulva that has been in or on your anus without thoroughly washing it with soap and water. Transferring germs that way can lead to serious health concerns.)

Myth #6. No woman wants to have a quickie.

Anything that starts with "no woman" or "every woman" is likely untrue, because we are all as different as we are alike. Plenty of women enjoy quickies. Once again, it's all about the who, when, where, why, and how.

A quickie doesn't have to result in an orgasm. It can be a lovely tease to keep you on edge until you can satisfy that itch. It can also be a fun way to connect with your partner when there's no time for anything more.

Once again, when it comes to female orgasm, it's all about leaving your preconceived notions at the door, learning about what you like, and communicating that to your partner. Whether or not that includes quickies is all up to you.

Myth #7. *If you have a skilled partner, there's no need for sex toys.*

This is bunk. Period. Having an orgasm isn't easy for all women, and there's no shame in using whatever means you enjoy. So bring on the toys, and the more the merrier as far as I'm concerned.

One of my favorite things is to have a partner penetrate me slowly with Betty Dodson's Vaginal Barbell while stimulating my clit with any number of vibrating goodies.

Remember, it's not about the right way. It's about your way. And if your partner has an issue with toy use, you know what I always say—they know where the door is.

Myth #8. *All women can easily reach orgasm.*

Women are not men. I repeat: Women are not men. It generally takes us upwards of twenty minutes—at least—to have an orgasm, and that's when we're really both attending to ourselves and being attended to.

Intercourse is not the main event. (I know, I know. Scrape yourself off the floor.) The biggest problem when it comes to female orgasm is that men and women expect women to be able to come in the three to five minutes that most men last during penetration. But it doesn't work that way for most women. We need twenty to thirty minutes of clitoral stimulation on average, and a combination of activities is generally preferred—and still, there are no guarantees.

Forget hard and easy. It's not about what it takes. It's about wanting it and having it and doing what it takes to get there.

Myth #9. *Position makes no difference when it comes to female orgasm.*

Position makes all the difference when it comes to orgasm, but not for the reasons you might think. It is unlikely that a woman will come from penetration alone. If she does, it will be because everything prior to that was stellar, the penetration was well-timed, and the position allows for clitoral stimulation either directly or indirectly.

Position really makes a difference during sexual activities *other* than intercourse, because leverage and the ability to see what you're doing are so very important.

Myth #10. Penetration is the key for a woman to reach orgasm.

Intercourse alone usually does not lead to orgasm. Fewer than 25 percent of women say they can orgasm via penetration alone. Even that number may be high; most likely, those women who reported orgasm from penetration alone were experiencing some level of clitoral stimulation from the thrusting. I would argue instead that 99.9 percent of women need clitoral stimulation if they are going to reach orgasm. There are always the outliers. But we're talking about the rule here, not the exception.

Myth #11. Male orgasm is primary and female is secondary.

This, naturally, is the myth that burns me the most. If you have a male partner, this is the most important thing you need to know when it comes to orgasm: Yours is just as important as his. Equal.

Just because it may take you longer. Just because you can have more varieties, more often. Just because penetration alone doesn't necessarily do the trick for you. None of that means that female orgasm should in ANY WAY take a backseat to male orgasm.

It's no wonder that this myth has become so rampant. The penis is so obvious about its needs and its results. The pussy tends to be a great deal more subtle. Regardless, male and female orgasms are equally important. Always.

Note: The reality is that men and women take the same amount of time to orgasm when being "properly" stimulated. Women only seem to take "too" long because what's being "done" to them isn't doing anything for them.

The best way to combat myths, of course, is with the truth. That is why it is vital that we know and accept the truth for ourselves and share it with others. Only then can we empower women sexually the way they deserve.

This can be a challenge for sure since we've had years and years of misinformation, misunderstanding, and misguidedness. It's our job as members of the sex positive revolution to spread the good word.

The truth can be scary. It can shake our very foundation. But it can also set us wildly free, and that makes truth telling all the more worthwhile. Don't be afraid to ask. Don't be afraid to tell the truth. Don't be afraid to know what you know. We've been going against our gut for far too long when it comes to female sexuality. Let's leave for the myths for the history books and pave our sexual futures with the truth.

The Truths about Female Orgasm

Truth #1. All orgasms have one thing in common—intention.

They are all about thoughtfully considering a woman's body and how it works. They are about being conscious. They are about setting aside everything that we think we already know. They are about shifting the paradigm. It doesn't matter how men's orgasms work. At all. When it comes to a woman's orgasm, the only thing worth considering is the woman having it.

Truth #2. Women's orgasms should in no way take a backseat to men's.

The clitoris is not a stunted penis, as Freud once suggested. The vaginal orgasm—which for all intents and purposes does not even exist—is not a mature orgasm, while a clitoral one is not immature, as he also asserted. Orgasms can emanate from a number of parts of a woman's body. But the clit is orgasm central. For the most part, it requires stimulation—direct or indirect—in order to make the magic happen. That is the truth. Freud and all his lackeys were wrong, and Betty Dodson and Anne Koedt and all of their fellow warriors were right. Period.

Truth #3. Orgasm could actually be considered part three in a four-step dance.

There are four steps that make up the human sexual response—

excitement, plateau, orgasm, and resolution. Arousal can either be reflexogenic, meaning it's caused by physical stimulation, or psychogenic, meaning it's caused by reading or thinking about or seeing something.

Becoming wet and swollen can be an excellent indication of excitement.[2] The clitoris and labia increase in size because the vagina has virtually no nerve endings of its own.. The nipples swell. Heart rate and blood pressure rise, breathing speeds up, and muscle tension increases. During the plateau stage, there is an additional increase in all of the above indicators, and the glorious sex blush begins to rise, making the labia appear darker, the clit retract, and the vaginal opening become more lubricated. The magical hormone oxytocin is released as well.

On average, women will experience three to ten contractions of the uterus and the muscles around the vagina at about 0.8-second intervals during orgasm, explained Dr. Justin R. Garcia, assistant professor of gender studies and director of education and research training at the Kinsey Institute for Research in Sex, Gender, and Reproduction at Indiana University, Bloomington, via an email interview on October 19, 2014. Generally these first contractions are doozies that are followed by less dramatic versions. As for resolution, women are the lucky ones because we don't have a refractory period or recovery phase, as men do, during which time orgasm is physically impossible. In other words, there's no reason not to dive in to round two before catching your breath from round one. Might as well enjoy the marvelous powers of the equipment we've been given! Although Dr. Garcia also added, "Some women will have hypersensitivity post-orgasm," so proceed with happy caution.

---

2   It's important to note that these are not always signs of arousal. According to Dr. Garcia, "Some women experience vaginal lubrication and even orgasm during rape—point being, orgasm is not always a result of wanting sex or orgasm or being in the right mood. The lubrication can be an autonomic response (and in fact may prevent damage, such as excess vaginal tearing, during forced penetration). The arguments continue among sexual psychophysiologists about the influence of autonomic processes and whether it is more of a central response (meaning, the relative importance of local stimulation to the genitals)."

Truth #4. There's no "right" way to come.

When it comes to female orgasm, we've been sold a sick and woefully untrue bill of goods. When it comes to heterosexual intercourse, the only party likely to come is the man. Why? Because the vagina provides ideal lubrication and friction in the pursuit of male orgasm. But that same act does little for most women in the orgasm department. It might feel "nice." But on its own, it's not likely to cause orgasm. And yet, too many people believe it is the right way or the only real way to come. Well, I'm calling bullshit on that.

The only right way to come is the way that makes you come. So if you come by having your clit stimulated manually while you are being penetrated, that's the right way. If you like to use a butt plug or have your pussy eaten, that's the right way. If you have no interest in penetration, if you like shallow penetration, if you like penetration by a dildo or fingers or a fist but not a penis, all while having your clit stimulated directly or indirectly, orally, manually, or mechanically, that is all right and all good.

You don't actually need my permission to come in the way that works for you. But if you are looking for permission from the orgasm gods, I'm granting it. Come. Come as you are. Come as you like. But for god's sake, give up on thinking that there is one particular way that you "should" come and that it should be defined by male wants and needs. That model has done all women a dangerous disservice for far too long already. It's time to put an end to the madness.

Truth #5. There's no such thing as "taking too long."

The average woman needs twenty to thirty minutes of play to lead her to an orgasm. That timing depends on a million things. It depends on you. On your cycle. On your day. On your partner. On whether you are playing alone. On whether you are using a toy. On whether you just got home from work or have been watching porn all afternoon.

But regardless of who, what, where, when, why, or how, it takes as long as it takes, and no one should be looking at the clock unless engaging in a specific quickie activity.

It burns me that this is an issue that even needs to be talked about. But

I feel so sad when a woman apologizes and says, "I'm sorry I'm taking so long," as if it's some sort of burden to have the pleasure and the honor of being sexually involved with her. I wouldn't be there if I didn't want to be, and I want to enjoy every moment and every inch of her.

Your partner should be enjoying what he or she is doing to you as much as you are enjoying having it done to you. If that's not the case, there's a whole other problem at hand.

Don't apologize. Don't rush. There's nothing wrong with you. At all. And worrying about the time keeps you from being present and makes it even more unlikely that you'll come.

Truth #6. Every sound is good.

A big part of having an orgasm is making sounds. Breath sounds. Throaty sounds. Whimpering sounds. Yelling sounds. Whatever comes naturally to you. If you stop those sounds, you're stopping, or at least hindering, your orgasm, because you're stepping out of the present and into some headspace that's telling you, "Don't make that noise. You sound weird." Or, "Be quiet. Someone will hear you." (Unless, of course, Grandma is in the other room. Then bite that pillow, baby!)

Don't waste your time or energy on those thoughts. Make the noises that come naturally to you. And if none come, test a few out. Some women find that vocalizing can help bring on orgasm. Try some deep, loud, intentional breathing, sighing, or moaning. Practice when you're masturbating to make it seem less challenging when you're with your partner.

Remember, there is no Best in Show when it comes to orgasm. The only thing that's important is that you come, if that's the result you're after. So forget about how all those silly porn films sound or how your favorite actress sounded in your favorite sex scene. Nothing else matters but you and your orgasm. And no one is judging you. If someone *is* judging you, I would highly recommend—you guessed it—showing them the door.

Truth #7. Every position is good.

Having an orgasm is like a scavenger hunt. You look everywhere possible for it and you don't worry about how strange the places where you need to look might be. The key is that you or your partner be able to stimulate the parts that you want stimulated. That is all that matters. I'm going to say that again—*That is all that matters.* So forget about what the magazines tell you. Forget about how you look. Forget about everything except for what feels good.

If I'm already sounding like a broken record, I'm not going to apologize, because I'm glad. If you get only one thing from this book, I want it to be this: If it feels good (and it's legal and consensual)—Do it. Do it. Do it. Do it.

Truth #8. Every vulva is beautiful and unique.

Every woman's body is a marvel. Eight thousand nerves ending in that tiny little (or not-so-little) externally visible clit. That is a glorious, glorious miracle. We have to remember that when we inevitably start feeling insecure about what our vulvas look like.

In case your life experience hasn't led you to seeing very many of them, let me assure you, they are all incredibly different. Some are quite open. Others amazingly closed. Some pairs of lips are even and others have sides that are rather different from one another. Some vulvas are ruffled, as if covered in ribbons or feathers. Others are full of straight lines and symmetry. Some bloom without a touch. Some remain tightly wrapped until carefully opened. Some have a great deal of space between the clit and the vaginal opening. Others are built with very little distance in between.

They come in all colors. Pinks and peaches and creams and yellows and browns and blacks. They come in the palest palettes and the darkest hues. They come with a depth and breadth of color that is almost impossible to fathom without seeing it, and they come in nearly monochromatic tones, although opening those particular pussies often leads to a delicious color surprise inside.

Some open and swell and get wet at just the whisper of a touch. Others require more attention. Some are coy. Others bold. Most all are soft as velvet to the touch, although even the texture varies from vulva to vulva.

The point of this is to say, whatever yours looks like, there is nothing wrong with you. Nothing. And if you don't feel good about what's between your legs, it's vital that you make peace with yourself. Talk to a counselor. Spend some serious time looking at your vulva and readjusting your attitude toward her by reminding yourself that whatever you are comparing her to is arbitrary at best. There is no pussy ideal.

The ideal pussy is the one you have. The ideal pussy is the one that is loved by her owner. The ideal pussy is the one that gets lots of attention. The ideal pussy is the one the possessor takes pride in and cares for and brings to orgasm.

Vulvar shame is based on spending too much time looking at porn and not enough time looking at other pussies. Google it. You can see a zillion of them, and what you'll see is something marvelous. Not to get too sappy here, but they really are like snowflakes—no two are alike, and that's a good thing.

Do whatever you have to and take pride in your pussy. That is the first order of business when it comes to having your ultimate orgasm. And if someone has shamed you for how your pussy looks, remember, that's about the shamer, not about you. When people shame others, it's because they are ashamed of themselves.

At a sexuality conference I attended in Washington D.C., I had the lucky happenstance of spending some time with one of the other participants after the conference was over. We found ourselves deep in conversation about sex and sexuality, and I was sad to hear that she was wrestling with some issues around vulvar shame. I certainly understood. I mean, the messaging about pussies and what they're supposed to look like is not awesome. Porn stars shouldn't be the poster children for anything beyond sexual entertainment.

But it made me feel really sad, especially when I saw her vulva. It is beautiful and incredibly unique. It is feathered and ribbony and much like an intricate oyster shell. We spent the evening playing, and I got so much pleasure out of those unique lips. There is something kind of magical about a pussy you have to unwrap in order to get into.

I have adored every pussy I have had the pleasure to play with, and I feel honored to have enjoyed pussies so markedly different from my own.

My friend from the conference told me that our time together made a big difference in how she feels about what's between her legs. I hope that if you have any bad feelings about your vulva, you will find a partner or an experience (maybe a Bodysex workshop!) that will allow you to see yourself as your lovers do—beautiful and inviting and completely unique. The last of these is a good thing despite what the girly mags and dirty movies might portray. The time has come for pussy pride and power.

Truth #9. Every way you move your body is good.

Too much porn and too many mainstream movies with incredibly unrealistic sex scenes have left us with very strange ideas of what "sex" looks like. But there is no wrong way to pulse or pump or grind or writhe or arch or rub or whatever else you may do. This isn't performance art. What it looks like means nothing. What it feels like means everything.

All women are different. That's good. But it can also be a challenge. It means that we can't count on our bodies to do the things that other bodies do. Instead, we have to trust. We have to trust ourselves, our bodies, our partners, our tools, and our skill sets. We have to trust our desires and go after the pleasure that calls us, because orgasm is a right. We have a responsibility to exercise it.

Your body and mind and spirit deserve orgasms. But you have to show up in order to have them. You have to really, really be present and act intentionally. You have to know that we're all different, all our bodies all work differently, and, most importantly, much of the information that we've been given is wrong at worst and thin at best.

The truth is, there is no perfect position or way to move that will guarantee that PVI intercourse will bring on female orgasm. So stop looking. The search party has been called off. Instead, focus only on mutual pleasure. If there happens to be a position that can get some women there sometimes, great. If not, no matter. This isn't about intercourse. This conversation is about you discovering your ultimate orgasm, no matter the method. Period. So let your body take the lead for once and think about nothing but what feels good to you in that moment.

Truth #10. All fantasies are allowed.

Let me say that again. *All fantasies are allowed.* You don't have to think about the person you're with. You don't even have to think about sex. You don't *have* to think about anything. But what you do have to do is let your brain go where it wants to go. That is, where it wants to go when it comes to turning you on. No bills or body image stuff. Leave that at the door.

Now is the time for all things sexy. Whatever that means to you. How do you figure that out? Trial and error. Think about the last time you were really turned on. Where were you? What were you wearing? What did you see? Hear? Taste? Smell? Who were you with? Follow that yellow brick road to wherever it leads. A harem of beautiful women at your service. A gladiator that you've told to stand in the corner until you tell him to service you. Tables full of elegant desserts. Parades of exotic animals passing through the desert. Sexy couldn't be any more personal.

And maybe it'll be the simplest possible thing. I have an Australian friend who talks about what a thrill he gets from watching a woman undress. I think we forget sometimes that the tried and true are tried and true for a reason. He loves the thrill of unclasping a bra and watching the straps fall down over bare shoulders. He loves seeing a woman in just her knickers (as he calls them). He describes the sheer delight of seeing bare breasts or feeling a woman's pussy getting wetter and wetter. These are the visions that fill his fantasies. The only thing that matters is that the fantasy works for you.

Truth #11. Orgasms are good for your health!

There are plenty of reasons to have an orgasm. If you need more, here's a rundown of some of the purported add-on benefits of the Big O. (Note: I ran these by Dr. Garcia and he said that some of them remain speculative at best. So consider them as value added as opposed to sure things!)

- *It relieves stress.* Thank you oxytocin and dopamine release!
- *It keeps you connected to your partner.* Oxytocin—often referred to as the cuddle hormone—makes you feel bonded to the person who facilitated that release.

- *It relieves insomnia.* Another happy side benefit of oxytocin is that it's known for making you sleepy.
- *It relieves depression.* Orgasm releases endorphins, which produce euphoria. Done and done.
- *It alleviates pain, including cramps and migraines.* Studies show that orgasm can double a woman's tolerance for pain. The even better news is that orgasm is not an anesthetic. It's an analgesic, which means that it stops the pain without dulling your sensitivity.
- *It prolongs your life.* Duke University followed 252 people over the course of twenty-five years in a study (Palmore EB) that concluded that having sex more often causes one to live longer. Why? All of those happy hormones being released.
- *It stimulates your brain.* Orgasm causes increased blood flow to the brain!
- *It keeps you looking young.* The hormone DHEA (dehydroepiandrosterone), which is released during sex, is a powerhouse at repairing tissue, therefore causing it to look younger. And, yes, there is a study for that.[3] It was done over a ten-year period, in fact. Judges were asked to guess the ages of men and women who had sex regularly, and the guesses were consistently seven to twelve years younger than the participants' actual ages.
- *It's good for your heart.* As is any cardiovascular workout. But sex is usually a lot more fun. You can burn over eighty-five calories having sex for thirty minutes. Here's a little fun math for you—fifty thirty-minute sessions equals 4,250 calories burned. Hello, candy jar.
- *It improves with time.* The old adage is true: Practice makes perfect. But these rehearsals and recitals will be way more fun than practicing scales or performing "The

---

3   *The Proven Way to Stay Young Forever.* David Weeks, Jamie James. Hodder & Stoughton, 1998.

Entertainer." Sex gets better the more we play and the more comfortable we become with our bodies and our desires. So don't fight the urge. Give in!

* *It keeps colds at bay.* Regular sex has been shown to increase the body's levels of immunoglobulin A, an immune system booster that may just help the body tell the common cold to take a hike.

Truth #12. All women are different. Very different, in fact.

This likely will come as no surprise, but hopefully will come as some relief. From the ways our bodies are built to the things that turn on our minds to the experiences and histories that we have, we are all very different, and those differences very much affect our sexual responses. Orgasm can feel completely different and totally the same from one orgasm to the next and from one woman to the next.

There is a lot of misinformation out there when it comes to female orgasm. We are responsible for our own orgasms, and we are responsible for making sure we have all of the correct information. Once you have that, the ultimate orgasm awaits!

5

Our Bodies, Our Orgasms, Our Pasts, Our Self-Play

How Our Past Plays into Our Future

OUR FEELINGS ABOUT OUR bodies and our orgasms play no small part in the quality and quantity of our climaxes. And our sexual pasts are certainly a major part of that. Left unaddressed, our sexual pasts become our sexual destinies.

For some of you reading this book, your first O might seem like a very, very long time ago. You might not even remember exactly when it was. Maybe it was alone. Maybe it was partnered.

If it happened via masturbation, and you were a kid at the time, the way your parents, or other parties who were aware of your behavior, handled the subject can have a huge effect on your own feelings. All too often, parents "catch" their kids masturbating and chastise or punish them for the act. Sound familiar?

If you associate pleasure with "Don't touch that" or "Don't do that" or "That's disgusting," it makes sense that you might not have the best relationship with masturbation or orgasm.

The first time we have an orgasm with a partner—as well as the first time we have partnered sex, whether it is with or without orgasm—can also very much shape our understanding of and experience with orgasm.

If you had partnered sex for the first time and did not have an orgasm, and your orgasm, in fact, seemed to be of no matter to that partner, you may have, from that moment forward, understood orgasm to be some sort of privilege to be bestowed upon you at a partner's whim. Even if that belief is not present in your conscious mind, it may well be a part of your subconscious.

That being the case, it would be all too easy to adopt an attitude of "I get the scraps I get" when it comes to sex and pleasure. But that kind of thinking will get you nowhere fast. You have a right and a responsibility to your orgasm. This sort of thinking also easily lends itself to harboring shame about desiring orgasm.

It goes a little something like this: *My partner doesn't give a second thought to my having an orgasm. If I do, he will think I'm ridiculous or greedy or slutty or fill-in-the-blank.* And, just like that, you've fallen into the eternally spiraling shame trap.

But there is simply no place for that. There is simply no space for shame when you are building a healthy relationship with your orgasm.

Women have as much right to a healthy sexuality and kick-ass orgasms as men do. The problem lies in the fact that, as feminist writer Anne Koedt so eloquently put it in her 1972 essay "The Myth of the Vaginal Orgasm," "Many more women [are] simply afraid to establish their right to equal enjoyment, seeing the sexual act as being primarily for the man's benefit, and any pleasure that the woman got as an added extra" (Koedt 1972, 114).

But remember, your pleasure should be your partner's pleasure—and vice versa—no matter how it's achieved or what it looks like or sounds like. In other words, the "me, me, me" of porn is just silly entertainment. It should in no way shape your sexual reality.

The thing is, everyone has a story when it comes to our sexual histories. For some of us it reads like a fairy tale. For others, a nightmare. Some of our stories unfold just as we imagined they would. Others are far from anything we ever could have conjured. The one thing all of our stories have in common is that they affect who we become sexually, for better or for worse.

But although they affect us, they don't have to define us. Before we can dictate what our stories will mean, though, we have to see them for what they are and decide for ourselves whether it would be best to hold tight or let go.

Whatever your story, the one thing I can absolutely assure you of is that you are not alone. Women's stories of their first sexual experiences and orgasms range from the divine to the despicable to everything in between. And each story reveals something powerful and important.

It's not so much what the stories are about that is important, but what those stories can do to us if we allow them to become our truth. When things are left in the dark to fester, that's all they can do: fester. But when we bring them into the light, we can see them for what they are, empower ourselves with the stories that serve us, and release the ones that don't.

For most women, losing our virginity has at least somewhat molded who we have become as sexual beings, whether that molding was conscious or not. We learn who we are sexually based on the sexual experiences we have, starting with the very first time.

Some experiences trump earlier ones. But still, that very first time, the one that you define as the time you "lost your virginity," stays with you.

So what is the connection between the way one loses one's virginity and how that affects the development of one's sexuality? Well, in many cases, if a woman has a positive first time, then the road ahead is far easier than if it was less than ideal. And by "less than ideal" I don't mean rape or incest, necessarily, since that obviously would have a negative effect. A negative experience could also mean a boyfriend who was more of a "hit and run" and uninterested in her needs, or someone she trusted who then told the whole school.

Or maybe someone remained a virgin till marriage because she felt pressured to do so, only to find herself sexually incompatible with her partner. Or someone could even have what she would consider a positive first time, only to have a parent find out and react by punishing her with groundings and the like.

This recently happened with an acquaintance of mine. She found out that her mature, polite, straight-A, star-baseball-playing teenage daughter had sex, and now her daughter is permanently grounded and not allowed to play baseball. What's the message?

My point in all of this is to say that if you have a less-than-positive story, you have the power to reclaim that story. How you feel about orgasm is important. Really important.

Here are some questions to consider when thinking about your relationship with your orgasm:

What did it mean to you to lose your virginity?

Do you consider it an actual "loss," or would you consider the experience a gain of sorts?

Can you lose your virginity more than once? If so, would you want a do-over?

Do you consider your story to be positive or negative? Why?

How do you feel about orgasm?

Can you draw a connection between your sexual past and how you feel about orgasm now?

If you're game, doing some writing or journaling, or even simply jotting down some ideas, can be a great way to really think about and address these thoughts and ideas.

My point in all of this is to prompt you to think about why you may feel the way you do about orgasm, and to either expand on or remove yourself from that past depending on whether or not it's serving you. Without making that shift, it can be a huge challenge to make peace with allowing yourself to access the level of pleasure of which your body is capable.

It often times strikes me as very sad when I think about our communal attitudes toward female orgasm. It's an extra, an afterthought, an add-on. It takes an empowered and knowledgeable woman to have truly knock-out, ultimate orgasms, or even to get her needs met in the most minimal way.

The thing is, regardless of where you are with your orgasms, assuming we all want to land in the same place—regularly having stellar orgasms—the path is pretty much the same. Learn how your body works. Learn how to talk to your partner about how your body works.

As I mentioned earlier, I had an exceptionally positive first time, which I have since learned is highly unusual. It included all of the important elements: respect, empowerment, body acceptance, and being seen as a whole person.

If your first time did not have those elements, I'm hoping you have had such experiences since then. If not, now is the time to seek them out, because those, beyond any tips or tricks or techniques, are the key to having astounding orgasms.

Seeking out those experiences means only having sex with people who see you as an equal partner. And if those partners are men, they have to be men who see PVI sex as one sex act, not *the* sex act. This, unfortunately, can be challenging. Even the most enlightened, sweet, well-intentioned men have been known to accept the common and dangerous definitions of sex and sexuality that are so incredibly harmful to women and their sexual well-being.

As Koedt (1972, 112) explains, "What we must do is redefine our sexuality. We must discard the 'normal' concepts of sex and create new guidelines that take into account mutual sexual enjoyment.... We must begin to demand that if certain sexual positions now defined as 'standard' are not mutually conducive to orgasm, they no longer be defined as standard. New techniques must be used or devised which transform this particular aspect of our current sexual exploitation."

It's a big shift. I get that. But it's a worthy and valid one. Women are whole people. Women exist and have value, regardless of men and their existence and regardless of our relationships—sexual and otherwise. Women do not need men. Women can choose men. They can want men. They can desire men. But, I repeat, women do not need men. Sperm is needed to procreate. But a man is not something a woman needs.

And that's a good thing. That frees both sexes to choose sexual and life partners based on what they desire instead of on some need. That means that two complete people—two women, two men, a man and a woman—can come together and complement each other and once and for all throw all of that insipid, rom-com, "you complete me" crap out the window. It's fun to watch on the big screen. It's no fun when it plays out in real life.

But before you even begin looking for sexual partners to enjoy orgasm with, you need to know your own body and what kicks it into high gear.

Masturbation

When it comes to knowing your body and what makes it sing, there is no better route to discovery than masturbation.

It's amazing to me that we simply don't talk about female masturbation.

We talk about male masturbation. Movies, television shows, jokes, pop culture references. There is a near endless list of slang terms for men getting themselves off. We talk about teenage boys doing it, adult men doing it. Boys and men talk to each other about doing it.

But when it comes to women, it's near radio silence.

When I started masturbating as a kid, the only thing I knew was that it felt good. Period. I didn't know it had a name. I didn't know it was a thing. I certainly didn't talk to anyone about it.

As I got older, I realized the silence around female masturbation was a problem. A big one.

One day, while doing laundry, I asked a friend for a tampon and she balked.

"I have a pad," she said. "But no tampons."

"You out?" I asked.

"I don't use them."

"Really?" I said, trying to hide my surprise.

"I can't. I don't want to have to touch..." She paused. "Down there." She whispered it quietly, the same way my family whispers the word *cancer*.

"How do you masturbate?" I blurted out. She turned beet red. As if on cue, the buzzer for the dryer went off. I've never seen anyone as happy as she was at that moment, armed with an excuse to race off to rescue the clothes from the dryer and herself from the conversation.

Guessing that if she felt that way, other women in our neighborhood likely did as well, I booked a sex toy party that very day in hopes that it might provide some needed "enlightenment." That party, held just a few weeks later, proved to be the most successful one the consultant said she'd ever held. Those girls were just waiting for permission. They were waiting for someone, anyone, to tell them that touching themselves was not just okay, it was a survival technique that no woman should do without.

I can't help but wonder how many women are waiting for permission. Sure, there was *Sex and the City* and all of their Rabbit talk, and Good Vibrations and all of their workshops and products. But how many women are still living in shame, either not masturbating or feeling so guilty about it that it hardly feels worth it?

If you're wondering why any of this matters, I'll tell you. As I've outlined in the previous chapters, orgasms are good for you. And masturbation means no partner or drama required. Have a migraine? Masturbate. Feeling stuck creatively? Masturbate. Feeling blue? Masturbate. Can't sleep? Masturbate. Mired in stress? Low self-esteem? Sex drive in low gear? Chronic pain? Masturbation is good for what ails you.

It's also good for what doesn't ail you. It feels good to slowly tease yourself until you can't take it anymore. It feels good to rub or buzz or pound yourself into a full-steam-ahead frenzy. It feels good to get off and it's empowering to be able to do it for yourself. It's your equipment. There is absolutely, positively no reason not to use it.

Which brings me to my point—masturbation is really important.

It's vital to learn about your body, and it's paramount that every woman knows she doesn't need anyone else to bring her pleasure. You can "take care of business" all by yourself. No risk of pregnancy or disease or slut shaming or anything.

Think about it. If you're all hot to trot, you make choices based on what your body is craving. But if you can please your body, you can ease your mind. What if we made decisions about sex not because we wanted to get off, but instead because we wanted to connect emotionally and physically with a partner of our very specific choosing?

I know. I know. All too often, men use love to get sex and women use sex to get love, and if it's love that women are seeking, no amount of masturbating is going to fix that. But hear me out.

If a woman is feeling empowered by being able to pleasure herself; if she is feeling strong and confident and in control of her own body; if her stress level is low and her level of self-esteem is high; if her serotonin levels are soaring; she's going to be far less likely to give herself away sexually for acceptance or "love" from a partner, because she already accepts and loves herself.

This empowerment also allows women to take their time in finding a partner. "I have to get laid!" doesn't have to lead to dating the wrong person.

I'm the last person on earth who would sing the praises of abstinence. But I would be the first person to promote women not settling for crummy sex and nonexistent or mediocre orgasms.

Women are sexually hungry creatures. That's a good thing, and there's no reason to do without or settle. Masturbation can help keep us from having sex for the wrong reasons. But it can also teach us what it means to have sex in the right way—for us. As Betty Dodson explained in an email conversation on July 22, 2014, "Masturbation is the foundation for all of human sexual activity. It's how we first discover our genitals and develop positive sexual sensations by learning how to have orgasms. You must honor this often maligned sexual activity and see it as the most important love affair you'll have throughout a lifetime."

If you are not masturbating, it is vital to ask yourself why. If it's because you don't have a good relationship with your body, then there's no time like the present to commit to changing that. If it's about weight, talk to your doctor or a friend or a nutritionist or a trainer. Take a walk. Choose a healthier diet. If it's about other body issues, find a counselor or friend you trust and work through what's keeping you from loving your body.

It's yours. In some ways, it's all you've got. It's where you live, and you have to do whatever it takes to make it feel like home.

If you're not masturbating because you think there's something wrong with masturbation, it's time to let that go. There is nothing wrong with masturbation. It's as simple as that. If it's your religion that's causing the conflict in your head, know that you can still be a person of faith and masturbate. Lots of us are.

Your body belongs to you, and it was created with the ability to achieve great pleasure. There is no reason on earth not to relish and enjoy and take full advantage of that, regardless of what your religion might tell you. Keep in mind that many religious practices were designed to keep people in order, particularly women. It's time to get disorderly. No one—*no one*—has a right to tell you not to touch yourself, especially not a religious figure. You do not owe your body to your religion.

If you're not masturbating because your parents shamed you about masturbation, it's time to forgive and forget. They were wrong. Hopefully they were just doing their best to be good parents, and your sexual awareness just scared them or made them nervous or left them unsure of how to guide you. So maybe they told you not to touch yourself. Maybe they told you you'd go blind or get hairy palms or go to hell or whatever. Obviously none of that is true. There really is nothing more natural than masturbation. It is healthy and risk-free and can only do your body good. In fact, not masturbating is far more of a danger. Being pent-up and anxious and stressed and on edge are not good for anyone. Why would you suffer any of that when the solution is literally at your fingertips?

If you're not masturbating because you "feel weird" about touching yourself, you have to question where that's coming from. Friends? Movies? Books? News? Media? Whatever the cause, whatever the foundation for the weirdness, there is no reason to feel strangely about touching your own body.

If you're not masturbating because of a disconnection from your body, consider where that disconnect might be coming from. Body image may be one issue. Disability may be another, or a correlating one.

When it comes to sex and disability, it's vital to address the myths that often surround this subject. The following list is from *The Ultimate Guide to Sex and Disability* by Miriam Kaufman, M.D., Cory Silverberg, and Fran Odette, which is an excellent resource on the topic.

Myth #1 *People living with disabilities and chronic illnesses are not sexual.*

Myth #2 *People living with disabilities and chronic illnesses are not desirable.*

Myth #3   *Sex must be spontaneous.*

Myth #4   *People who live with disabilities and chronic illnesses can't have real sex.*

Myth #5   *People living with disabilities and chronic illnesses are pathetic choices for partners.*

Myth #6   *People living with disabilities and chronic illnesses have more important things than sex to worry about.*

Myth #7   *People living with disabilities and chronic illnesses are not sexually adventurous.*

Myth #8   *People living with disabilities and chronic illnesses who have sex are perverts. (Kaufman, Silverberg, and Odette, 2007)*

These things simply are not true. People living with disabilities have the same sexual needs and rights as anyone and deserve to be empowered and treated equally in that arena. If disability is something that you or your partner are living with, consider reading *The Ultimate Guide to Sex and Disability* or otherwise seeking guidance or counseling. We all have our roadblocks. But there is no roadblock that can't be addressed.

Humans deserve pleasure. Neither age, race, sexuality, disability, nor otherwise should compromise that. Period.

Masturbation is undeniably important when it comes to maximizing orgasm, for one simple reason—it allows you to know what does it for you. It allows you to discover what feels good. Where? How long? How hard? How soft? Fingers? A vibrator? Penetration? Rubbing against something? Something firm? Something smooshy?

There's no audience when you masturbate. (Unless you choose for there to be one, of course, which is actually an excellent idea. Having your partner watch you masturbate allows them to see *exactly* what you like.) You can masturbate exactly how you like and not be concerned with how you look. (Not that you should be concerned about how you look when you have partner sex. But god knows, it's hard not to think about it at least a little!)

If you masturbate, but not regularly, try getting more regular about it. The more you come, the more you'll want to come. The more you do it, the better at it you'll be. The more you explore, the more new things you'll likely discover when it comes to what you like—and don't like. And the more you get your brain in the zone, the more fantasies you'll be able to come up with for use during partnered sex.

If you find that it can be difficult to get your head in the game when it comes to self-pleasuring, there is nothing in the world wrong with spinning yourself a few juicy tales when you get down to business, whether it's alone or with a partner. Erotica can provide some great inspiration, and so can woman-positive, sex-positive porn. There is no shame in fantasizing. It's just your mind at play. Think Vegas showgirls or dirty cowboys or doctors and nurses or werewolves and cowboys. Whatever does the trick for you. (For more on fantasy, see Chapter Eleven.)

If you don't masturbate, try getting into the practice a little at a time until it feels like second nature to you. These tips will help get you off the ground.

1. Sleep naked. Get used to feeling your own skin. Don't be afraid to run your hands down the length of your body and linger between your legs. Your body belongs to you. You have every right to touch it.

2. Take a bath or spend some extra time in the shower. Remember, the idea is to get familiar with your own body and allow it to enjoy the sensations of pleasure that you are fully capable of producing all on your own.

3. Grab a mirror and have a look between your legs. If you have never really looked before, it's time. You may be shocked or scared or even a little put off by what you see. But there's no need. Look. Really look. Your pussy is part of your body. Your pussy is yours. Your pussy belongs to you. And your pussy is all good. No matter the size or shape of your lips or clit or hood or vaginal opening. You just have to trust me on this. It is all wonderful and beautiful.

4. Touch yourself. Gently. Quietly. Carefully. Timidly. Whatever it takes to get you started. Begin with your legs slightly parted and simply massage and rub and touch and explore the parts of you that are exposed. When you are ready, spread your legs farther apart. And, finally, part your outer lips and explore your inner lips and your vaginal opening. Rub and massage and play and dip your fingers inside.

   There is no wrong way to masturbate. Do what feels good. Avoid what doesn't. You don't have to come if you don't want to, and you can come over and over, as many times as you like, if that's your desire. So much in life is about so many other people—work, family, even going out; there are always other people's needs and desires to be considered. Not now. Masturbation is just about you. You. So enjoy.

5. Try a toy. A vibrator can be a great way to give yourself an orgasm. There are wonderful sex-positive, woman-positive shops all across the country, from Babeland in New York City to She Bop in Portland, Oregon, to Good Vibrations in San Francisco, where you can get advice about finding a toy that will suit your needs. There are plenty of places online as well. My favorite beginner vibes include the Form 2 and the Little Chroma from Jimmyjane, the Cuddle and the Adventure from OhMiBod, and the Lily, the Gigi 2, and the Ina Wave from Lelo.

If you are a regular masturbator, keep in mind that when you play alone, it can be too easy to shortchange yourself and go for the quick come. In order to avoid doing that, treat yourself the way you would treat a partner. Go for the tease. Enjoy your body. Try something new. Don't rush. Think in terms of the Push-Pull method that I discussed in Chapter Three. Push yourself as far as you can go and then pull back and repeat.

If you want to improve or change up your masturbation practice, you might want to check out Betty Dodson's Rock 'n' Roll method, which is ideal for staying focused and going for the best orgasm, not the quickest. The steps of the Rock 'n' Roll Method go a little something like this:

1. Relax on your back, bend your knees, and allow your legs to fall open and to the sides.

2. Massage your vulva with plenty of oil (almond, for example). Don't be shy. Massage the oil into your lips generously.

3. Begin paying close attention to your breathing. Breathe in and out deeply and slowly.

4. When you feel relaxed and ready, begin to slowly penetrate yourself with a dildo or vibrator. (Betty's Vaginal Barbell is great for this practice. It's weighted so it stays in place, and it has perfectly placed bulbs and ridges.) First insert just the end. "Observe the space you are entering," Betty advises.

5. Squeeze and release as you slowly penetrate. "No expectation," Betty suggested during the Bodysex Workshop I attended. "Remember, this is a muscle. Not a hole."

6. Begin to manually stimulate your clitoris. Small circles or an up-and-down motion or anything in between. Experiment until you find something that feels right for you.

7. Rock your pelvis up and inhale. Then rock down and exhale. Continue this pattern as you masturbate.

8. Begin using a vibrator, starting on a low setting. Do not begin directly on the clit, and do not leave the vibrator on the clit. Tease yourself, using the vibrator on your outer and inner lips, eventually coming to your clit and then moving away and coming back again.

9. Continue breathing rhythmically and rocking your pelvis.

10. If you feel an orgasm coming, pull back. The goal is the tease.

11. When you can't take it anymore, give in. Follow it. Stay
with it. Let it take you where it wants to go for as long as
it wants to go.

Here's the thing: I have no hard evidence on this. But I trust what I know
anecdotally better than I would trust any study. Women who masturbate regularly are more at ease. They are less stressed. They have better
skin. They are less anxious, less depressed. They sleep better. There's a
whole movement afoot called Orgasmic Meditation, or OMing. It's basically having a partner rub the upper left quadrant of your clit for fifteen
minutes. They say it works wonders, and I don't doubt it.

I imagine that it works because it's about no particular goal, just pleasure. Having someone else masturbate you is great and can be incredibly
bonding and fulfilling. (Although I do find it sad and ironic that you have
to create a movement to get men to do what lesbians have been doing
forever. Sit between her legs and focus on her clit. It's not rocket science.
It's just biology. Still, if it takes workshops and kits and classes and a name,
fine. Whatever it takes to get women's pussies the undivided attention
they deserve!)

I gave it a try with a past partner and it was really interesting. I don't
know that we followed the rules exactly. It was hard not to follow her
lead when she got more and more worked up. But it felt really amazing
to take care of her in that way. It was all about intention. Since the goal
wasn't orgasm but instead connection and grounding and focus, it felt
much more like ministering and much less like fucking, which was cool.

After doing it, she of course was ready to get to it, and when I told
her that wasn't really the point, she yielded but said it felt weird to be left
hanging. Later, though, she said it felt really good to connect to me like
that, and we both could see how it might work as a powerful daily practice. Although, again, it wasn't markedly different from how we usually
engage, other than the logistics. I had my clothes on. She had her top on.
The major difference was the intent.

The truth is that when we have sex, there are many different possible
intentions. To fuck. To make love. To make up after a fight. To soothe

one or both partners. I think to empower and to engage are equally valid intents, and using the principles of OMing could be a valuable way to do that.

But even more important is your ability to do that for yourself. If you don't believe me, do a little experiment. For one week, set aside fifteen to thirty minutes a day and masturbate. You can orgasm once or ten times or not all. Whatever suits you that day. But do it every day. Take note of you feel throughout the day. How your body feels. How alert your mind is. How aware you are of every sensation, from sight to sound to smell to taste to touch.

You know when you have a new sexual partner and the world just seems like a better place? Food tastes better. You find yourself humming along to every tune. The fragrance of that honeysuckle down the street suddenly wafts your way every time you walk past. It may be love. But I would bet money that more than anything, it's the orgasms.

It is wonderful to get involved with someone. Absolutely. It's fun and exciting and you feel so deeply connected. Ever wonder why that's so strong at the beginning? So insanely powerful that you can hardly eat or sleep? It's the orgasms. The orgasms have hormones racing through your body and telling you how elated and bonded you are.

And that's great. But it also can be a little confusing. Ever wonder about all those lesbian U-Haul jokes? You know: What does a lesbian take on a first date? A U-Haul, because lesbians have a bad habit of immediately moving in together right after meeting. That's because you have two women high on oxytocin from all the orgasms!

They may well be in love, too. But they can't possibly know if it's the real thing yet. That's what has girls chasing after boys who are no good for them but who seem like a dream come true in the moment. Orgasm is a powerful, powerful drug. It's a not a drug to take lightly. It's a wonderful high, but it can also cause you to make decisions that you would not otherwise make. So just remember that love may not be the only thing you're feeling.

All of that being said, why wouldn't you dose yourself, without the complication of a partner, when the perfect, legal drug is literally at your fingertips? Seriously, masturbate. And, again, if you don't believe me, just take the one-week challenge and see how you feel after treating yourself to a week full of those heady, happy hormones.

The point of all of this is to say that you need to be comfortable in your skin and know what it is that brings you pleasure if you are going to find your ultimate orgasm. You can have orgasms on your own and with a partner. But they aren't about finding a magic spot or perfect position. They are about knowing what you like and giving yourself permission to do it, or to ask for it, as well as to enjoy it. And if your past is holding you back, now is as good of a time as ever to decide you're ready to let it go. If you need professional help to do that, seek it out. There is no shame in that.

If it's simply that past experiences, your first or otherwise, or your upbringing or religion have left you in the lurch, talk to a friend or start taking small steps to letting your past be your past and embracing what you can make of your sexual future. No one has a right to that but you.

These are our bodies, our orgasms, our pasts, and our self-play, and taking ownership is the only way to lead ourselves to our ultimate orgasms.

6

Orgasm Gets Social

THERE'S NO EXCISING THE ROLE that society plays in orgasm. Society doesn't belong in the bedroom. But somehow it always sneaks its way in. It makes sense, really. Society is us, no matter how much we might not want that to be true, which means we cannot ignore how society affects our orgasmic lives and how our orgasmic lives affect how we fit into and move around in society.

For better or for worse (more likely worse), unless you have some really awesome parents—which I am thrilled some people do!—school is one of the first places we learn anything that even remotely resembles sex education, barring Google and porn. One of my survey takers posed an interesting question about just that, asking how we can incorporate orgasms into sexual education. She writes,

> I came from a fairly liberal community, and our sex ed included putting a condom on a banana, but we [only] learned about ovulation, menstruation, [male] ejaculation, and conception. Our entire sexual education was learning the mechanics of procreation, to which the male ejaculation (which was never referred to as an orgasm) is integral.
>
> But that leaves all pleasure—for both parties—out of the equa-

*tion. Even the people who want to teach "abstinence only," do we not
assume that these kids will eventually grow up, get married, and
have God-approved sex? By the time they reach that level of commitment, are they not several years removed from sex education?*

*I lost my virginity when I was in high school, but not only did I
not have my first orgasm until I was twenty-four, but I didn't know
that I wasn't having orgasms, because I had no clue what to expect. It
wasn't until...a partner who was several years older than myself told
me that just "being really wet" does not mean having an orgasm [that
I realized]. If we teach kids about how to really pleasure both male
and female sex organs, it incorporates empathy and intimacy into their
education of the practice of sex. Why is that not already a part of it?*

I love this question so much. Why don't we talk about orgasms in sex
ed? That's simple. Because we're terrified. Because we live in a culture of
fear and scarcity when in reality we have a world of beauty and bounty
at our feet.

We don't teach kids about orgasm because having an orgasm is about
having autonomy over one's body, and we are too busy teaching kids to
sit still and memorize what we tell them for the test.

We don't teach kids about orgasm because we are so frightened of
pleasure. And why is that? Because society, and more than anything religion, wants control over us and what we do and how we live.

We don't teach kids about orgasm because in the name of creating a
civilization, in the name of creating civility, we created sterility instead.
We have cut ourselves off from our bodies and our senses, and we have
forgotten how to really get in there and really feel every little sensation
that we as humans are privileged to enjoy.

When was the last time you rolled in the grass, or stood at the edge of
the sea and let the sand swallow your feet, or shouted out to the trees as
you ran through the forest?

To my mind, it's going to be a very long time before we ever teach orgasm
in school. So we're going to have to start at home. We have to tell kids

that there's nothing wrong with masturbating. We have to tell kids that sex feels good and that's good. We have to tell kids about orgasms and not tell them silly fables about hairy palms and burning in hell.

What are we teaching? Well, according to a State Policies in Brief Report from the Guttmacher Institute titled "Sex and HIV Education" (Guttmacher 2011):

- Twenty-two states and the District of Columbia mandate sex education
- Thirty-seven states and the District of Columbia require school districts to involve parents in sex education
- Eighteen states and the District of Columbia require that information on contraception be included
- Thirty-seven states require that information on abstinence be provided; twenty-five of those require that it be mandatory.
- Nineteen states require school districts to teach that sexual activity is only appropriate within marriage.
- Twelve states require discussion about sexual orientation

There are no requirements, of course, about teaching pleasure or orgasm or anything other than *Don't get knocked up, don't knock anybody up, and don't catch anything.* Depressing, I know.

The mountains may be impossible to move. But we can take baby steps toward them every day. Tell the truth. Tell yourself the truth about your amazing body and what it can do and feel, and tell your kids the truth too. All in age-appropriate steps, of course. But tell them.

Our education about sexuality is so incredibly important. It forms how we see sex and orgasm, and what our rights and roles are in relation to that. All too often, men who crave sex and orgasms are "just being guys," but women who have the very same desires are deemed selfish or whorish. One survey taker wrote:

I feel like the orgasm has been kept in the man's world and a man's orgasm is more discussed and investigated. I just want men/science to know more about them! Our sexuality is key but is often ignored. I want younger women to know their orgasm matters as much as a man's orgasm does. Besides, why would so much emphasis be placed on male orgasm when they can usually just have one, while we can go on indefinitely?

This issue is as simple as it is complicated. So many things affect our sexual attitudes—history, religion, politics. Not to mention that men are bigger and stronger and so historically their wants and needs and desires have been put first. Women are sacred vessels to be protected, and boys, well, boys will be boys.

It's ridiculous and it's time that it be over. Women have to take charge of their sexuality, and they have to refuse to sleep with men who continue to perpetuate this dangerous myth that somehow male orgasm is better or more important than female orgasm.

We're talking about sexual pleasure here. There's no need for hierarchy. Though the questioner here is correct in wondering why the gender that can have *one* is held in higher esteem than the gender that can have *many*. But that's just more of that cultural idea that boys are generally bigger and louder and stronger and so what they have or do is the best and everything else falls behind or beneath that.

So what are we to do? Well, we can start with these four steps.

- Step one: Move PVI from center stage. It is one sexual act. Not *the* sexual act.
- Step two: Don't sleep with men (or women) who don't value your orgasm. Just don't.
- Step three: Spread the good word. We have to talk about our sexuality. We have to share with our partners, but also with our friends and family, when it comes to giving information.
- Step four: Don't participate in shaming. Sex is good.

Women who have sex and like sex are good. Drop the acts. We're not virgins or whores. We're women with healthy desires, and we deserve to have them satisfied. When that becomes the accepted norm, everything else will fall into place.

Our cultural attitudes don't just affect partner sex; they affect our orgasms and our masturbation practices and our relationships to our bodies. I've got lots of practical tips later in the book, but I feel like one thing has to be addressed before we even begin this orgasm conversation in earnest. It has to be said. Women as a whole don't masturbate enough, and that directly and negatively affects their orgasmic lives. The reason why they don't is all too simple and all too sad: shame and misinformation.

There are still women who think that their bodies are gross or that their private bits are gross or that they don't have every right to feel and to give themselves pleasure.

As I discussed earlier, masturbation is like a magic medicine cabinet. It can relieve pain and stress and help you sleep. You can do it any time you like, and it's easy once you give yourself permission to do it and enjoy it.

All I know is that if you don't masturbate, if you're afraid to or too ashamed to, now would be a great time to read up on it, talk to supportive friends about it, address what's stopping you, and take a step toward making a change.

If you've never looked between your legs, take a peek. It's an amazing sight. If you've never touched yourself or tried a vibrator or rubbed against a pillow or read erotica or taken advantage of that hand-held shower massager, take some time for yourself.

It's your body.

Perhaps the biggest issue that this book is going to raise is how to be a fully empowered, fully self-actualized, fully orgasmic woman and find a partner that can live up to your new orgasmic expectations. If you are looking for a female partner, it will be easier—hopefully, anyway—because you don't have the male stereotypes and expectations and socialization issues to wrangle with. Hopefully, you will both want to be fully orgasmic people and you will each want that for one another.

But if you're a woman looking for a male partner, you are going to face some challenges and some opposition. This is a vital point to address, as you will most certainly have to be mindful of it as you move toward finding your ultimate orgasm.

A friend very eloquently summarized this issue, so I'd like to share here what she said.

> *I feel a sort of struggle as a sexually empowered woman to find a man that can "play with that" and not be intimidated or just not get me. If I stay true to that and to what I know I should be able to expect from a partner, it feels like I will be alone a lot more than if I'm willing to settle. So how do you give women a language to voice the new paradigm of what they can expect from men, and also, how do they feel juicy/ sexually satisfied while they wait for a good partner to play with (assuming the screening process will make it more difficult with the higher expectations)?*

First of all, trust that it is worth the wait. Women do not have to settle for mediocre partners. Ever. Second, masturbation is your friend. Use it to satisfy yourself. Use it to learn what you want from a partner. Use it to build sexual self-esteem. Use it to buy yourself however much time you need to find someone who "gets you" in bed.

Now to the bigger part of that question—a voice for the paradigm shift in expectations. That's as easy as it is hard. You have to tell the truth. You have to say, "I want an equal partner in bed." You have to say, "I expect to come more than you do because that's what my body is capable of." You have to say, "There's no place for ego in my bed." You have to say, "I trust and respect and desire you enough not to fake it." You have to say, "PVI is not the main attraction for me. It's not the main attraction for most women."

I know that probably sounds nuts. And I'm not suggesting this as some sort of exact script. What I am suggesting is that you become comfortable with these thoughts and ideas and then work to make the language your own. Einstein once said that the definition of insanity is doing the same thing over and over and expecting different results. We have to start working toward different results. We have to stop doing the same thing over and over in order to do that.

Language is a vital tool in the battle to accomplish equality in the bedroom. We have to talk to our partners about our desires. We have to talk about embarking on an adventure of sorts in order to discover our own ultimate orgasm. We have to say we won't settle. In the end, that's better for everyone—men and women, straight and gay. No more faking it. No more ego. No more feeling like a failure. No more crazy expectations. Just a level playing field where we can all seek our sexual pleasure and where we can all ultimately find it.

Imagine if men were told that PVI sex was bad and that the main event was for them to have a woman lie on top of them and rub her clit on them. Nothing more. Just that. And if they couldn't come from that, well, then there must be something wrong with them, because that's what sex is. That would be ridiculous, right?

But if women continue to have sex with men in ways that don't make them come; if women continue to fake it; if women continue to put their partner's ego above their own pleasure; if women continue to remain silent about their desires; then the sex they are having will continue to be as subpar as it has been in the past.

I'm going to generalize here for a minute, so bear with me. I know this isn't true in every case. But based on my experience, to my mind, it would be great if women approached sex with men the same way women approach sex with other women. When women have sex with one another, they explore what feels good and what makes them come. There isn't one single act that defines lesbian sex. It is circular rather than linear. It is highly mutual.

Heterosexual sex, on the other hand, feels like a setup for failure for women in so many ways. Anything but PVI is treated like a bothersome add-on, even though PVI rarely gets women off on its own, especially in the three to five minutes it generally lasts. And then the party is over unless he offers to "finish her off," which generally makes a girl feel like she's asking for something extra. Then she has to fake it or feel lousy for not coming, and he feels like he did great (assuming he buys the fake orgasm). Or his ego is deflated if he doesn't buy it or she doesn't fake it.

All of this is doing men as much of a disservice as it is doing women. Men could be having much better sex and much more sex if they followed the lesbian model, with lots of manual and oral stimulation, plenty of kissing, and some penetration thrown in there. She could come and then he could come and then she could come again and again, and if enough time passes to cover his refractory period, he could come again too. In other words, take PVI off center stage and the show can go on a heck of a lot longer.

This can be the new paradigm. All we have to do is support it. We have to speak it. We have to make it our truth and not have sex when it falls outside of this model. If you want to get laid, you have to be willing to play in this new way. Change is hard. People hate it. People will hate me just for saying all of this because it calls into question everything they have previously known to be true.

But who cares? Too many women aren't having the great orgasms, the ultimate orgasms that they have a right to. They are missing out. They are selling themselves short, and if they aren't standing up for their inalienable orgasm rights, then they have no one to blame but themselves.

All you have to do is say the words. The best part is that it's an incredible litmus test. Any partner, male or female, who is open to seeing sex in this new light is a keeper. Anyone else, well, here's your coat, here's your hat, don't let the door hit you on the way out.

Too many women continue to cling to a desire to come from penetration alone and wonder, "What is wrong with me?" when in reality, the only thing that is wrong is the perception that PVI sex is the end-all be-all sex act. It may be for most men. But it certainly is not for women.

Sex has to be about mutual pleasure. It has to be about exploring what works for the people involved. It has to forgo all previous models and start from the basics. Great orgasms come from understanding your own body, sharing that information with your partner, and having sex that may or may not include PVI intercourse but that certainly and intently focuses on the thing that brings a woman actual pleasure—the clitoris.

It's time that female orgasm takes its rightful place alongside male orgasm and stops playing second fiddle. Just because most men can come quickly and easily from a very obvious and simple act does not mean that their orgasm is any more vital than ours. It just means that they have been lucky enough to live without society telling them they shouldn't touch themselves or enjoy sex or do the very things that give them pleasure, and they should instead do things that leave them frustrated and unfulfilled.

Anne Koedt (1972, 114) says, "Looking for a cure to a problem that has none can lead a woman on an endless path of self-hatred and insecurity." Well, that's basically how things are for women. People were raised and trained to believe that procreation was the primary goal of sex, and one of the best ways to procreate involves PVI sex, so PVI sex became the main event. And because it served men and men have been and continue to be in roles of power, it remained the main event. It served them, so why would they change it?

As Koedt (1972, 113) explains, "We are living in a male society which has not sought change in women's role." But the day of reckoning has arrived. Women are tired and frustrated and bored. Straight women and lesbians alike—because even in some lesbian relationships there is a desire to imitate heterosexual behavior, because it is what we are taught is "normal."

It's time, though. It's time to let all of that go. There is simply no reason for a woman to sleep with a man if his focus is on PVI sex. Why bother? You can be frustrated all alone; you don't need a partner for that.

The truth of the matter is that women did not—and in many ways still do not—have a voice that is heeded in society at large or in the bedroom. Even worse, some women don't even have a voice or feel that they deserve to have a voice. If we don't have a voice, we cannot proclaim ourselves sexual beings and if we don't proclaim that for ourselves, then no one else will. If we are not sexual beings, than our orgasms don't matter and don't get studied or discussed. It's an ugly dangerous cycle and it all begins with not being considered whole, individual humans separate from men.

"Sexually a woman was not seen as an individual wanting to share equally in the sexual act, any more than she was seen as a person with independent desires when she did anything else in society. Thus it was easy to make up what was convenient about women; for on top of that, society has been a function of male interest, and women were not organized to form even a vocal opposition to male experts" (Koedt 1972, 115).

The issue is with the pervasiveness of the message, the insistence that female orgasm is secondary. Why else would there ever be articles like "How to make her come in three minutes"? Unless it's about the fun of quickies—which is not ever what those articles are about—it is demeaning to women to imply that the goal is to get us to hurry up and come so that the male partner can get to the good stuff, the real stuff, the actual sex.

"Foreplay is a concept created for male purposes, but works to the disadvantage of many women, since as soon as the woman is aroused the man changes to vaginal stimulation, leaving her both aroused and unsatisfied" (Koedt 1972, 113).

This is definitely one time when heterosexual women would be wise to take a page from the lesbian book on sexual attitudes. For lesbians, the only goal is mutual pleasure. The menu is open to anything the women involved want to involve themselves in. There are no preconceived notions about how to have sex. There is no reason to stop, ever, because there is no refractory period to wait out.

It would be great to kick society and all of its expectations and implications and socializations out of your bed. And you can, in some ways, because you get to be the boss of your body and your bedroom and your orgasm. But, unfortunately, in other ways, you simply can't ignore the world at large and how it affects you and all of the reast of us. So, instead, what I present to you here is a framework to be able to find your ultimate orgasm while still living on this planet, on the grid, with the rest of us, It's good for men and women both. As Betty Dodson explained via email, "We are constantly protecting the male ego, and it's a disservice to men. If a man has any sensitivity or intelligence, he wants to get the straight scoop from his girlfriend."

You can stay true to yourself and still have an incredibly orgasmic life. But only if you are willing to advocate for yourself and not just accept what society doles out to you. Society doesn't get the final word. Religion doesn't get the final word. Your lovers don't get the final word. You and only you have that luxury. Don't squander it.

Bread and Butter:
The Clitoral Orgasm

The Scoop

I KNOW YOU'RE HERE for the how-to. But bear with me here for a moment. It'll be worth the read. Trust me.

When it comes to ultimate orgasms, clit awareness is paramount. And this may come as a surprise to you, so brace yourself: The exposed part of the clit is just the tip of the apparatus whose sole purpose is pleasure. Yup. It's just the very tip. The rest is nestled inside you, prepared to thrill at will.

Clitoral stimulation makes women come. Bottom line. Do some women come without it? Perhaps. But unlikely. Does it matter? Not at all. The truth of the matter is, there are lots of other yummy parts to explore, but the clit remains the main player in this game.

Think of all the rest—which we'll get to in the next few chapters—as ancillary zones and not the primary zone, and you'll find yourself a lot more satisfied. And you'll be giving yourself a lot fewer reasons to self-flagellate for "failing," since these add-ons were never meant to be the main event.

If you want a surefire way *not* to orgasm as a woman, focus on the ancillaries like PVI. PVI can be great. It can create intimacy. Slow penetration can feel wonderful. Sometimes hard and fast can feel great too. But although it might be a main course for men, it's a side dish for women. PVI is procreative, and it is generally much more effective at providing men with orgasms than it is women.

Sex and intercourse are not synonymous. Intercourse is one item on a glorious menu. One. Because men are in the position of power, and have been for far too long, it has become *the* menu item, the main course, the big event. But it shouldn't be. At all. There is a long menu of activities when it comes to ancillaries, of which PVI intercourse is one.

This isn't about unseating men. Not at all. In fact, it's about empowering men and women. I can't imagine how exhausting it must be to do something over and over and wonder why it never quite works.

In her famous orgasm manifesto, "The Myth of the Vaginal Orgasm," Anne Koedt (1972, 116) wrote, "The recognition of clitoral orgasm as fact would threaten the heterosexual *institution*. For it would indicate that sexual pleasure was obtainable from either men *or* women, thus making heterosexuality not an absolute, but an option. It would thus open up the whole question of *human* sexual relationships beyond the confines of the present male-female role system."

We are going to reclaim sex as human-centric instead of male-centric, and we are going to start telling the truth. Women come via clitoral stimulation. There is lots of other fun stuff that can go on, and lots of it can feel really good. But it's all ancillary. All of it.

Part of the problem is that many women don't even know their own equipment, and so it can be easy to fall prey to the idea that PVI or penetration is the only game in town.

So you're going to need to know what you're dealing with down there in order to get to that ultimate orgasm. Your ultimate orgasm. Here's a friendly little owner's manual to getting to know and using your equipment.

First, I want to clarify something here. The words *vulva* and *vagina* are not interchangeable. *Vulva* = external. *Vagina* = internal canal. You don't want to confuse the two, because the two are not interchangeable or comparable. The first provides pleasure. The second is a vessel. And any pleasure that comes from the vessel is actually from the internal legs connected to that external beauty, the clit.

What you see on the outside of your body is your vulva. Not your vagina. The inner canal is the vagina. It gets way too much attention simply because that's the part we know and talk about.

The clit is situated at the top of the vulva at the meeting point of the inner labia. The tip, which is what is visible from the outside, sits beneath a hood and is home to more than eight thousand nerve endings. Its sole purpose is pleasure. Get it revved up, and it swells and becomes more prominent.

But there is much more to the clit than meets the eye—literally. The entire clitoris is shaped like a wishbone, with legs that sit on either side of the vagina and stretch out in the direction of your thighs. Too many women think that the clit is only that tiny visible tip, which is a shame, because that means they have sex without knowing what they should be stimulating—and how—if they want to come.

The truth is that the clitoris is as impressive an organ as the penis. But it boasts far more nerve endings and can be stimulated in a plethora of ways, internally and externally. It's a tidy piece of equipment that gets short shrift because it does not cut the imposing swath that the penis does and instead waits patiently within.

In fact, according to a conversation via email on August 12, 2014 with Dr. Joanna Ellington, author and reproductive physiologist, "Female erectile tissue ('the clitoris') that responds to sexual arousal is a large struc-ture lying on either side of the vulva, deep to the labia, from the mons to the rectum. The exact size and shape differs somewhat between women; just as the penis (the correlate in men we can see) differs man to man."

This is not secret information. But not enough women—or men for that matter—know it. This is where a great deal of confusion comes from when the issue of vaginal orgasm arises. There is no vaginal orgasm. As Koedt (1972, 112) explains, "Women have thus been defined sexually in terms of what pleases men; our own biology has not been properly analyzed. Instead we are fed the myth of the liberated woman and her vaginal orgasm—an orgasm that does not in fact exist."

The vagina is not the highly sensitive body part that too many people imagine it to be, Dr. Garcia of the Kinsey Institute explained via email October 19, 2014. It doesn't even require anesthesia for certain medical procedures because of its lack of sensitivity. And yet it got all the glowing attention, and the clit was pushed aside as some little blip.

But because of the shape and placement of the clitoris—the hidden bits of it, that is—many people think it is the vagina itself that is aroused when it is, in actuality, the clitoris, Garcia continues. Why is this important? Because we have to let go of our attachment to the vagina.

Garcia explains, "In fact, the clitoral organ is much larger than the clitoris glans—the visible part. The entire organ wraps around the frontal vaginal wall, and some scientists believe that during vaginal penetration the stimulation of the underbelly of the clitoral organ contributes to orgasm experience and intensity." The point of all of this is to say that all women are different. Our bodies are built differently. Our clits have different levels of sensitivity. Our experiences and backgrounds and desires and interests are all different. But there is one thing that is the same:

The clitoris is the center of a woman's pleasure. No matter how you cut it. No matter how much religion or society or history or male ego might get in the way. The facts are the facts and the clit is where it's at. Period.

There are many, many ways to stimulate the clitoris to orgasm. Penetration can be a component of that. But it is far from necessary and far from top of the list. This can be threatening to men. I get that.

Koedt explains this beautifully and without apology.

Men fear they will become sexually expendable if the clitoris is substituted for the vagina as the center of pleasure for women. Actually, this has a great deal of validity if one considers only the anatomy. The position of the penis inside the vagina, while perfect for reproduction, does not necessarily stimulate an orgasm in women because the clitoris is located externally and higher up. Women must rely on indirect stimulation in the "normal" position.

Lesbian sexuality could make an excellent case, based on anatomical data, for the irrelevancy of the male organ. Albert Ellis says something to the effect that a man without a penis can make a woman an excellent lover.

Considering the vagina is very desirable from a man's point of view, purely on physical grounds, one begins to see the dilemma for men. And it forces us as well to discard many "physical" arguments explaining why women go to bed with men. What is left, it seems to me, are primarily psychological reasons why women select men at the exclusion of women as partners. (Koedt 1972, 116)

So, if it is men that you prefer as sexual partners, understand that you may have a bit of a battle ahead. But it's a winnable one in which both parties come out the victor. No longer do your male partners have to feel like failures. Instead they can become massively evolved heroes by learning your biology, listening to your needs, and following the ways of the lesbian lover where desire and pleasure, as opposed to societal norms and old habits, lead the way.

The clit is the center of female orgasm. Focus on stimulating that and forget about everything else you've come to know about sex, and you'll find your ultimate orgasm. Trust me.

The Practice

When it comes to orgasm, everyone has an opinion. But don't be fooled—just because someone is a doctor or ran a test or did a study or has lots of letters after his name, it doesn't make him an expert. The only thing that matters is you and your orgasm. If it feels good to you, it's right. Period. And for the majority of women, what feels really good is direct, external clitoral stimulation.

Keep in mind that no one can "give" a woman an orgasm. A woman has an orgasm. It is not something that someone grants to someone else. It is something that you give yourself over to. Don't get me wrong; another person can certainly help to facilitate your having one, and it is vital that you harness that power and take command of your role in having an orgasm. That is the path to ultimate orgasm.

Power resides in you, which means you can also play with it. For example, you can give the control of your next orgasm over to your partner, vowing not to come until you're "allowed," if you're game for a little power play. That can be very exciting, as long as it remains what it is—play. It only works if you are comfortable enough to allow your partner that power. If you're with someone who is merely taking it, that makes them the scary kind of controlling partner that you should avoid. Remember—enthusiastic consent is key to every sexual activity.

There are four primary ways to stimulate the clit: manually, orally, electronically, and, for lack of a better term, rubbing.

Manually

The clit likes to be wet when it is being stimulated. So when you begin with manual play, have your partner draw the wetness from your vagina onto your clit or use a little lube.

There are so many ways to engage the clit. It is mesmerizing to me how differently women like to be touched. But here are a few ideas to share with your partner to get you started.

- Begin by massaging the outer lips and running your thumb up and down the introitus (opening) of her vagina.
- Slowly make your way to her clit and experiment with a variety of ways of engaging it. Begin by gently pulling back her hood to expose her clit. Then gently rub her clit, paying close attention to her breath. Listen for sounds and watch her hip movements for indications of whether she is enjoying what you are doing. (Keep in mind that some women may not give you any indications, and you may need to ask directly.) Here are some ways you can play with a woman's clit:
- Make small circles.
- Pinch gently.

- Pull gently.
- Move two fingers from side to side.
- Grasp the clit (within the hood) between your thumb and forefinger and slide your fingers up and down the length to "jill her off" (the equivalent of jacking off a guy).
- Make a fist and run your fist up the length of her introitus to her clit and down again. Spend more or less time at her clit based upon her response.
- Fold your pinkie and ring finger down and put your middle and index finger at her introitus and your thumb on her clit. Using a pinching motion, bring your fingers together and pull ever so slightly out and back in a stroking type motion. Repeat over and over, varying the motion, angle, speed, and pressure, asking her as you do which variation feels best.

Orally

Cunnilingus is a magical thing. Pussies love warm, wet mouths and curious, persistent tongues, and clits love to be licked, sucked, bitten, and otherwise devoured orally. There is no right way to give head. But here are a few tips to share with your partner about how to give you the kind of tongue-lashing that will leave you begging for more.

1. Turn off your internal timer and cover up any visible tellers of time. Going down on a woman should have no time restraints—unless that's part of the game. Otherwise, both giver and receiver should simply melt in for as long as the pleasure is mutual.
2. Use long broad strokes from the bottom of her introitus to the top of her clit. When you reach her clit, suck, bite, lick, and tease. And then repeat.
3. Suck her clit, varying the intensity and pattern.
4. Lap at her clit.
5. Use your tongue to snake through all of her lips and folds,

       stopping to suck, lick, and bite as you go. Remember, the outer and inner lips are super sensitive too. So don't let the clit have all the fun.

5. Draw the alphabet with your tongue. It might sound silly and it's definitely old-school. But just because it's a classic doesn't mean it doesn't work. I like to do lowercase, then uppercase. It keeps the pattern varied and it's a great way to get your girl juiced up.

6. Use your whole face. Bury your nose in her clit. Enter her with your tongue. Then run your tongue over her introitus and up to her clit.

7. You may also want to slip a finger or two inside her vagina and use a come-hither motion or move your fingers like you would your legs if you were kicking through the water.

In other words, have your partner enjoy you. That's the point. Have your partner lie between your legs, arms underneath your thighs, to pull you into his or her face and mouth. Or straddle your partner's face and grind your pussy into his or her mouth. Place a pillow under your backside to protect your partner's neck.

Now, if you're shuddering in horror at that last thought, hang on just a moment. I have a confession. I found it really challenging to do at first, too. I couldn't imagine that a partner would want me all over her face. But then, I love having a woman's pussy all over mine. So why wouldn't she feel the same way?

Even those of us who consider ourselves highly sexually liberated have doubts at times about some sexual acts. That's perfectly normal. But it's also the perfect time to challenge and stretch ourselves to break the arbitrary boundaries that keep us from our ultimate orgasms.

Shame is a sad and dangerous thing. The world gives it to us and we have to fight it. I'm not saying it's easy. Not at all. I'm just saying it's vital to own it and overcome it rather than accept it as our truth and miss out on the world of pleasure out there just waiting for us.

HAND JOBS ARE FOR WOMEN TOO!

Felice Newman does an amazing job of mapping out manual stimulation in The Whole Lesbian Sex Book. Here's her advice:

Begin by massaging her inner thighs, butt, and outer labia. Snap on latex gloves, add plenty of water-based lube, and open her lips. Notice the glans of her clitoris. Has it retreated in its hood? Is it erect? How big is it? Are her lips engorging under your gaze? What color are they? Do her inner labia protrude from her outer lips?

Stimulate her entire vulva—outer labia, inner labia, perineum, the opening of the vagina—before you concentrate on the body of the clitoris. Run your fingers through her pubic hair, or, if she's shaved, stroke the silky bare skin of her outer labia. Ask her which of your caresses she likes best. Pay attention to her responses—both verbal and nonverbal.

Many women prefer indirect stimulation until they're extremely aroused. They may like caresses to the side or just above the clitoral glans. With arousal, the clitoris becomes erect and swollen and can take a lot more direct stimulation.

Your partner may like small circles traced lightly over the glans with just the tip of a forefinger, or a back-and-forth rubbing motion on the side of the clitoral shaft. She may like to feel two fingers sliding rapidly on either side of the clitoris. She may like you to press firmly on her mons with one hand as you stroke her clitoris with the other. Many women enjoy clitoral stimulation combined with vaginal or anal penetration, (Newman 1999)

HOW TO GIVE NEW MEANING TO "BEING A CUNNING LINGUIST"

I love this list of techniques from Violet Blue's *The Ultimate Guide to Cunnilingus* (Blue 97-99). So I wanted to be sure to share it with you!

- *Cover her vulva with your entire mouth.*
- *Nibble the outer and inner lips, or the clitoral hood.*
- *Use your tongue in different ways; it can be soft, light, and pointed, or it can have a focused and firm tip.*
- *Learn to use the ice cream lick to your advantage. Make your tongue flat and wide, and lick her vulva like a melting ice cream cone.*
- *Try sucking her clitoris.*
- *Try gently taking her clit in your teeth and holding it, lightly flicking with your tongue.*
- *Penetrate her vagina (or anus) with your tongue.*
- *When your mouth makes full contact, try moaning appreciatively—your mouth and tongue will vibrate her vulva, a delicious sensation in itself. If you're not shy, hum a tune.*
- *Lick lazy circles around her clit. Lick side to side or up and down, nipping with your lips between directions.*
- *Use short, rapid upward strokes, alternating with dipping into her vagina.*
- *Lick in circles combined with open-mouthed embraces.*
- *Alternate between circles and side-to-side licks.*
- *Run your tongue back and forth across her inner lips, then use gentle suction on the lips.*

- *Use the same technique on the clitoris.*
- *Alternate small, focused circles on either side of the hood.*
- *With your tongue tip, lick in the furrows from top to bottom, pressing in gradually with each stroke.*
- *Lick, plunge in; lick, plunge in.*
- *Start with "ice cream" licks up and down, followed with down strokes with your fingertips or flattened thumbs.*
- *Swirl your tongue in the space between her hood and mons, and rub the outer labia with flattened fingers.*
- *Lick ABCs on her vulva. Start with A and go from there—capitals, lowercase, cursive, secret messages. This method is an old standby.*

Electronically

There is nothing in the world wrong with using a vibrator. Using a vibrator will not ruin you for any other sexual stimulation. Using a vibrator does not imply that there is anything wrong with your partner's skills. Using a vibrator does not mean there is anything wrong with you and your ability to orgasm. Using a vibrator will not cause any sort of long-lasting numbing effect.

Vibrators are great because they don't get tired and they don't lose track of the rhythm you are enjoying. They can offer a pressure and speed and consistency that no human can. They are great for masturbation. They are great for partner sex. And there is no reason in the world not to use one. There should never be any shame or embarrassment about using one. They are great tools, and I guarantee that anyone who has issues with you using one is just dealing with his or her own issues. And that's no reason for you to have to worry about that.

There are many, many vibrators on the market that are great for clitoral stimulation. Workhorses like the Magic Wand and the Mystic Wand are classic standbys. I myself prefer something more like Jimmyjane's Form 2 or Lelo's Lily. But even a simple bullet can do the trick when it comes to clit stim. The trick is to find one whose shape, texture, pattern, and speed you like.

When using a vibrator for clit stim, start off to one side and stimulate your clit through the hood before going straight for the good stuff. Otherwise your clit may protest! Too much too soon is not a good thing.

Once you are good and warmed up, then you can move to direct clit stim. Now comes the fun part! Play with placing the vibrator on different parts of your clit. Try holding it still as well as moving it around. If the vibrator has a number of pattern settings, try out each one. Move through the speeds—slowest to fastest—and see which suits you best and for how long.

Vibrators can be great fun with partner sex. Hand the reins over to your partner or try out a remote-control version. There's even one from OhMiBod called blueMotion that you can control using an app on your phone. The point of sex is to have a good time, and if a little electronic help can make that happen, there's no reason not to indulge.

As author expert Jude Schell explains in her book *Her Sweet Spot: 101 Sexy Ways to Find and Please It* explains, "Tools can crush limitations, alleviate performance pressure, and amplify the action" (Schell, 105).

Via email conversation on August 15, 2014, Schell elaborated on this in a way I really appreciate. "The vibrator endures for many as a favorite accessory, yet no one enhancement, whether alone or with a lover, should be deemed indispensable. Any tangible or intangible requisite for a climax can inhibit a true exploration of a woman's vast capacity for pleasure."

And there are lots of resources online, so you can get the assistance you need and the anonymity you might want. No worries there. But remember, buying sex toys is nothing to be ashamed of. Check out Good Vibrations, Babeland, She Bop, Jimmyjane, Lelo, OhMiBod, and other sex-positive, woman-positive shops and brands to get both the guidance and the support you need.

THE RIGHT TOOL FOR THE RIGHT JOB!

"In all your plotting to introduce erotic toys into your sex life, remember that the toy is merely the utensil to help you whip up a tasty sexual feast....Use the following guide to make the right toy selections," offers Violet Blue.

Sex Act	Right Tools for the Job
Masturbation fantasies, her	Slimline vibe, dual-action vibrator, bullet vibe, wearable finger vibe (variable speed vibes a plus)
Masturbation fantasies, him	Cock ring, masturbation sleeve, vibrating penis cup, Fleshlight, lubricant
Anal play	Butt plug, vibrating anal wand, anal beads, dildo, and always lubricant
G-spot play, female ejaculation	Firm, smooth, curved dildo or vibrator and lubricant: can be glass, metal, hard plastic, or firm jelly rubber (variable speed vibes a plus)
Strap-on sex	Easy-on harness, lubricant, dildo
Threesome fantasy with two people	Dildo with suction cup base that attaches to wall, chair, or floor; sex machine; or harness that straps a dildo onto furniture or a pillow
Sexual power exchange	Restraints; sexual wearable such as nipple clamps, anal plug, or chastity belt; blindfold; ball gag; remote control vibrator; teledildonic device
Being sexually "used"	Sex machine; face or body harness with dildo; extreme restraints; sex sling or swing; sex furniture; collar and leash
Bondage	Ropes, cuffs, arm and leg bindings; blindfold; bondage travel kits (sold at specialty BDSM stores); feathers and soft fabrics—or spankers, riding crop, whips

(Blue 2006, 28)

Again, if shame is an issue, that is certainly understandable, but it is no reason to stop yourself from living. It just means that you absolutely must work through the shame, whatever that means for you—professional help, reading books, talking to friends and family—and rise above it to live as your full authentic self. Otherwise the shame and the shamers win.

Rubbing

Clits love to rub against things. Furniture, pillows, warm thighs, other clits; anything, really, that will allow them to rub long and hard and rhythmically enough to get off. There's no shame in rubbing one out. So take advantage of your surroundings and your partner's body to treat your clit to the simplest and often one of the most enjoyable ways to get off.

Position yourself however you feel most comfortable against whatever or whomever you choose to get off on. Again, this is one of those times when you may feel embarrassed about doing such a thing in front of a partner. But you'd be amazed at how many people tell me they love watching their partner get off by rubbing.

Many women love watching their partner's body move, her pelvis thrust, her whole body engaged. And they especially love it when they are the object to be rubbed upon. And, there is nothing like the sensation of opening your wet pussy, positioning it on your partner's hip bone, and riding it until you simply cannot take it anymore.

You might feel like you're just using or taking advantage of your partner. But talk about it. You will likely discover that your partner doesn't mind a bit, because it's you doing it and your partner loves you and desires you and wants you to experience pleasure in as many ways as possible!

The clitoris is a glorious apparatus, and we as women are incredibly lucky to have them. The clitoris is the founder of all orgasms. And she is not just a tiny external tip. She is a long, leggy structure with an internal presence that could give any penis a run for its money when it comes to length. Not to mention more than twice the nerve endings!

Relish the clitoral orgasm, because it is your orgasm. Crafting it into your ultimate orgasm involves discovering what kind of combo you most desire in order to find the blended orgasm that most women crown as ultimate. And that will likely change depending on the day, your mood, your partner, or your choice to play along. Just remember, the clitoral orgasm is your bread and butter. The rest is the trimmings. Not required, but definitely worth exploring and sprinkling in at will!

8

Orgasm 2.0:
The G-Zone, Female Ejaculation,
and Squirting

The G-Zone
The Scoop

I'M AS HESITANT AS I am excited to tackle the G-Zone conversation, and I'll tell you why. It's not a spot, and it is. I know, I know. I'm supposed to be making this easier, not more difficult. But bear with me here.

First of all, from here on out, I'll be referring to it at as the G-Zone rather than the G-spot, since it's not quite as specific as some might have you believe. The thing is, it's in there. The other thing is, it might not do much for you, and that's okay.

There is an area inside the vagina that is composed of highly sensitive spongy tissue. The G-Zone is comprised of three things: erectile tissue, glands, and ducts. In many women, it is two to three inches from the vaginal opening (one-third of the way to the cervix, or about two knuckles in), tucked behind the pubic bone—in and up, actually, on the vaginal wall's anterior (the front side, toward the belly).

Here's what's interesting. Dr. Joanna Ellington, an internationally recognized scientist in the area of sexual medicine, explained via email on August 12, 2014, that studies of MRI images and cadavers do not identify a separate structure from the rest of the clitoral cluster, which includes all female erectile tissue: the clitoris, distal urethra, and vagina (or the clitorourethrovaginal complex). In other words, these are all connected, and they all respond to stimulation, much as the shaft and the head of the penis both respond to sexual stimuli.

So it's all the same. It's all the clitoris. It's all erectile tissue. And it's all different. It's all zones and bits and parts. But ultimately, it all works together.

The reason I'm a bit hesitant to discuss it is that people have a habit of putting far too much emphasis on finding and stimulating it, to the point where women feel bad about themselves if they don't feel aroused by it, and anyone who can't find it or stimulate it feels bad as well.

Here's the thing. It is there. But it's not some magical stand-alone entity. Once again, it is part of the clitoral structure. But it is not a required stop on the Orgasm Express. It's an optional stopover, and it's up to you to decide whether or not it's worth devoting time to.

I personally recommend at least checking it out. What's the harm? You may discover something that makes you feel amazing. And if not, well, nothing ventured, nothing gained.

If you're wondering where the name came from, you can thank Dr. Beverly Whipple and Dr. John Perry for that. Whipple is a certified sexuality educator, sexuality counselor, sex researcher, and co-author of the international bestseller *The G Spot and Other Recent Discoveries About Human Sexuality,* which has been translated into twenty languages and was re-published as a classic twenty-three years later, in 2005.

She and her colleague named it after Dr. Ernst Gräfenberg, the OB/GYN who created the first IUD. He had written a paper about the sensitive area we now commonly call the G-spot, as well as about female ejaculation. Remembering when she first began writing about the spot, Whipple says, "A friend said you should call it the Whipple Tickle." Instead they decided to name it after Gräfenberg. "I feel really good that we named it after him," she says. "My publisher shortened it to G, which some people mistook for *Gee!*"

She says in her work, authored with four additional experts, that the

G-spot "is probably composed of a complex network of blood vessels, the paraurethral glands and ducts (female prostate), nerve endings, and the tissue surrounding the bladder neck.... It is the clitoral urethral complex. There are so many areas that make up the G-spot, not just one tissue. It's not on the vaginal wall. But it can be stimulated through the vaginal wall."

The truth is, women actually possess a great deal of erectile issue in their bodies. Whipple continues,

> *The G-spot is a sensitive area felt through the anterior wall of the vagina about halfway between the back of the pubic bone and the cervix, along the course of the urethra. It is easiest to feel the G-spot with the woman lying on her back. If one or two fingers are inserted into the vagina, with the palm up, using a "come here" motion, the tissue that surrounds the urethra will begin to swell. When the area is first touched, the woman may feel as if she needs to urinate, but if the touch continues for a few seconds longer, it may turn into a pleasurable feeling.* (Jannini et al. 2010)

The urethral tube, which lies on top of the vagina, is surrounded by the G-Zone. Sexual arousal causes swelling in the tissue, making the G-Zone particularly noticeable. As Betty Dodson explained to me via email on July 22, 2014, "A woman's vulva is heavily endowed with erectile tissue. We have nearly as much erectile tissue as men, but ours is internal, except for the clitoral glans plus the inner and outer labia."

How does an orgasm with G-Zone involvement feel? One survey taker described it like this: "G-spot is a very specific orgasm. It's usually with a toy that has a rotating head, and I'm on my knees straddling it and grinding into it. If positioned just right, it'll hit the spot, and a very intense and powerful, pressure-filled orgasm erupts."

Otherworldly is my favorite way to describe it. It's not as intense as an orgasm that involves anal play or A-Zone arousal. But it is big and full and tends to last through a number of iterations. I find it challenging at times to differentiate between an incredibly long orgasm—up to thirty minutes of that "Oh my God, I think I might die" action that results from using a dildo or having my lover's fingers inside me, as well as a second vibrator (or my lover's tongue or fingers) on my clit—and multiple orgasms which come in wave after wave. Not that it matters, really, since no one is asking me to check a box clarifying my orgasms! But it is clear to me that blended is best. That's when I have my ultimate orgasm.

It bears mentioning that some women have begun signing up for a procedure that claims to enhance the G-Zone. Collagen is injected into the area in order to enlarge it. It's basically the same deal as having your lips plumped, although instead of looking good, feeling good is the goal. The idea is that the plumping makes the zone more sensitive and thus increases the ability, the intensity, and, perhaps, even volume of orgasm. This is an interesting theoretical possibility. But I'm not buying it just yet. After all of my research, nothing convinced me that it was a real possibility. I did consider getting it done myself, in the name of research, but the danger for me far outweighs the possibility of any benefits. What if numbness was the result? Not worth it. Enough said.

The G-Zone, then, is another lovely area on a woman's body that may enjoy being stimulated. It is not, however, some sort of magic button that you just press and *voila*—an orgasm. That does not exist. I repeat: That does that exist. That does not mean that the G-Zone does not exist. It does. The question is—what does it do for you, and what has to be done to get it to do that for you?

The Practice

If you want to do a little G-Zone research, have your partner insert two fingers into your vagina, curve them up and into the zone, and execute a slow and repeated come-hither motion, adjusting speed and pressure and location based on your feedback.

The more you play with the G-Zone, the more juiced up with fluids it becomes. It will swell, giving it an impressive firmness. Once it gets good and worked up, orgasm will likely follow, possibly with ejaculate.

This is definitely one of those all-hands-on-deck, participatory exercises. You need to be wet and ready, and your partner needs to be of the "seek and explore" ilk rather than the "search and destroy" if you're going to get anything out of this exercise.

If you're really in it to win it, here's my step-by-step plan for discovering and exploring your G-Zone.

1. Remove any clocks, phones, or other devices that keep track of time. This is not the time for timing.

2. Make sure you have secured whatever level of privacy makes you feel comfortable. Kids at Grandma's. Roommates out of town. Music or fan on to cover sounds. Windows covered. Or not. Whatever will keep your mind from leaping to "What if…?", take care of it.

3. Get on the bed or on the couch or on a cozy pallet on the floor. This is about being somewhere where your body is comfortable.

4. Keep the lights on. Looking and being looked at is sexy. Adjust the blinds, light the candles, dim (or turn up!) the lights. Make it as bright as you feel comfortable with. Are you seeing a theme here?

5. Lie on your back with a pillow under your head and one under your hips. Bend your knees and let them fall naturally to the sides. I know what some of you may be thinking. "Am I at the gynecologist?" "That's too weird." "I don't feel comfortable being that exposed." I hear you. But I'm also going to tell you this. Your partner wants to see you and enjoy you, and if she or he doesn't—you know what I'm going to say by now—get rid of the bum.

6. Have your partner use lots of oil or lube and massage your vulva. No feathery fingers here—a real, full-on juicy massage.

7. Once you are amply jazzed up—that is, your clit is hard and your outer lips are swelling—have your partner slide

two fingers inside you. They only need to be a few inches inside—the texture of the G-Zone will be apparent, and it will make itself more known as you become more aroused.

8. Have your partner use an "up, in, and down" or "come-hither" touch to tease the G-Zone, following your lead for speed and pressure.

9. The best use of the G-Zone—like the best use of all of your zones, really—is in combination with other zones. So, tell your partner what other parts you would like to put into play. This can include sucking on your clit, using a vibrator on your clit, teasing your ass with her fingers… you get the idea.

10. Have her or him keep it up for as long as you can stand it, and then allow yourself to give in.

11. Allow the orgasm to come. Don't hold back, even if you feel like you have to urinate. If you emptied your bladder prior to playing, you most likely do not have to urinate, and you may well be about to squirt. This is the point where you have to simply trust your partner and your body and let go.

THERE'S NOTHING TO BE AFRAID OF!

To get the full scoop on the G-Zone, read the article "Who's Afraid of the G-Spot?" Here's an excerpt.

To stimulate the G-spot during vaginal intercourse, the best positions are the woman on top or rear entry, so the average penis will hit the anterior wall of the vagina [21]. Some women describe experiencing orgasm from stimulation solely of the G-spot. The orgasm resulting from stimulation of the G-spot is felt deep inside the body, and a bearing-down sensation, similar to a Valsalva maneuver, during the orgasm is commonly reported [3,22]. Physiologically, the orgasm from G-spot stimulation is different from an orgasm that is produced by clitoral stimulation. During orgasm from clitoral stimulation, the end of the vagina balloons out. During orgasm from G-spot stimulation, the cervix pushes down into the vagina [3]. Many women experience a "blended orgasm" when the G-spot and the clitoris are stimulated at the same time [3]. However, it is important to note that not all women like the feeling of stimulation of the G-spot area.

As has been written in the final chapter of the first book on The G-spot, if G-spot stimulation feels good, then women should enjoy it, but they should not feel compelled to find the G-spot. This is not a goal that women and their partners should strive to achieve [3]. Women need to be encouraged to enjoy what they find pleasurable and not set up finding the G-spot or experiencing orgasm or female ejaculation as a goal. People need to be encouraged to regard the G-spot as one area of sensual and sexual pleasure that some women enjoy. (Jannini et al. 2010)

As Whipple herself notes, the blended orgasm, for the majority of women, is truly where it's at. When you combine internal and external stimulation, you can craft an orgasm that many, many women would describe as ultimate. One of my favorite ways to play is on my forearms and knees with my partner entering me from behind with the Cuddle, a curved G-Zone–focused vibrator, while using the Form 2 on my clit. Holy smokes.

Squirting and Female Ejaculation
The Scoop

Some argue that squirting (or what some people call gushing) is not the same thing as female ejaculation. The thing is, the "experts," the scientists, and all the regular girls like you and me out there doing field research are still on the fence about female ejaculation and squirting (if they are different) all around. By the most commonly accepted definition, female ejaculation is when the female prostate emits a thick, whitish fluid. Squirting emanates not from the prostate, but instead from the bladder, and releases fluid that is—don't freak out—basically diluted urine.

Here's the biology. The Skene's gland can be found on the back wall of the vagina. It's located close to the lower end of the urethra. In some women it could be near or even a part of the G-Zone. That, of course, explains why G-Zone stimulation could result in female ejaculation. It's also the reason it might not do a damn thing for you at all.

In "Who's Afraid of the G-Spot," the authors explain, "Some women experience an expulsion of a small amount of fluid (about 3 to 5 cc) from the urethra with G-spot orgasms (as well as with orgasms resulting from stimulation of other areas). The fluid produced by this 'female ejaculation' has the appearance of watered-down, fat-free milk. It is chemically similar to seminal fluid but is different from urine [17, 23–25]. Researcher Milan Zaviacic conducted hundreds of studies on autopsy specimens and concluded that the fluid is from the paraurethral glands, which recently have been named the 'female prostate gland' [26]" (Jannini et al. 2010).

Since these are two different phenomena, that would explain why some people say the fluid released when a woman squirts has urine in it and some say it doesn't—because these are actually two separate phenomena and two separate fluids.

It is incredibly important to keep in mind that great orgasms aren't necessarily about being with a great lover. They are about being with a great listener who listens to what you desire and follows your directions. When it comes to orgasm, it's not about knowing the most, it's about listening the most.

So if your partner is dwelling on seeing physical evidence of their sexual prowess, tell him or her to step off. This isn't about your partner. It's about you. If you ejaculate or squirt, good on you. If not, it really couldn't be any less important. Emissions do not indicate orgasm. The strongest orgasms can hit with no emissions at all.

There were definitely some squirters among the women I surveyed. Many of the women who had not squirted expressed a desire to, and some of the women who had squirted felt some level of guilt or self-consciousness about it. But the majority of them found it pleasurable at best and entertaining at least. And some, naturally, simply thought they had urinated in the bed or on their partner.

So can and do all women ejaculate and squirt? No and no. And who cares? Just because you have the parts doesn't mean those parts will operate in the same way as they do in other people. I have legs, but they can't run a marathon. I have hands, but they can't paint a masterpiece. I have a brain, and it's great with words and terrible with numbers. To make matters even more complicated, some scientists argue that some women are born without the Skene's gland. So there's that. But back to the important bit here—who cares, really?

Trust me, you're not missing anything. Whether you ejaculate or not, whether you gush or not, whether your orgasm originates from in, out, or around, all pleasure is good. I've said it before, and I'll say it again: the goal is to find your zone, your pleasure, your desire, your max. This is no time for comparison.

All that being said, there's nothing wrong with squirting—at all. It is a perfectly natural, normal physiological response. Any guilt or shame is societally based and something we must all work collectively to abolish.

Is it messy? Sure. But sex is messy. So put a waterproof pad on your mattress or throw down some towels before you throw down, or get yourself some Chux (those blue lined pads), and you're good to go.

Sex has gotten too tidy, and I blame the media for that. But we only have ourselves to blame if we internalize those images of perfectly tousled hair and Instragram-worthy O-faces and bodies that look like photo-shopped catalog page content.

Sex is loud and messy and exciting and funny and silly and outrageous, and it's not a spectator sport. It's meant to be played. Hard. It's a lot like dancing. You sweat and move and follow the rhythm, and you always have a much better time if you worry less about who's watching and more about how your body is feeling.

So, squirting is nothing to be embarrassed or concerned about. The fluid is perfectly innocuous, and two seconds of planning before the fun ensues can minimize any mess you might be concerned about. And once again, if you have a partner who is crazy enough to be offended by your glorious body working in its glorious ways, it's time to start recasting for the role of the person lucky enough to have sex with you.

Now, it also bears mentioning that squirting is not the black belt of sex. It is not a badge to be earned or a pinnacle to be reached. It does not make the squirter a higher-level sexual human, and it does not make the squirter's partner a sexual legend in his or her own right.

All orgasms are good. Some are stronger or longer. Some are different from one another. But they are all good. The soaking wet ones are good. But they are no better than the ones that come sans gusher.

Knowing what works for other women and what other women experience is great. (Heck, it's one of the reasons I wrote this book!) But sex is no time for comparing yourself to other people—especially porn stars. You've heard it before, you're sure to hear it again. Porn is not real. Porn stars are not real. They are fantasies to some and nightmares to others.

So keep in mind, just because you see it in porn does not make it real. In fact, if you see it in porn, it probably is not real. So if a female porn star "ejaculates" or "squirts" on film, it's possible that it's real, yes. But it's also likely that what you're seeing is actually a woman peeing or a woman whose vagina was filled with water prior to penetration to make it look like she's gushing.

Famed sex educator Betty Dodson argued in our email conversation on July 22, 2014, "The biggest problem with 'squirting' or female ejaculation is that most people think it's the same thing as having an orgasm. It is NOT an orgasm, but it can accompany an orgasm depending upon the individual woman. It became overly popular in the online porn that is standing in for sex education in America. This is a serious problem because porn is basically entertainment for men. It does not speak to women's needs and desires."

In men, the urethral tube does double duty, delivering both urine and semen. Some argue that it's the same deal with female ejaculation. None of this—female ejaculation or squirting—has to do with lubrication, of course, as that happens inside the vagina.

Although some argue that there are methods to "make" a woman ejaculate or squirt, I'm going to have to call bullshit on that. You can be part of facilitating an orgasm that emanates from the G-Zone and thus may result in squirting, and you can be part of facilitating an orgasm that leads a woman to ejaculate. But the word "make" should really be removed from the discussion about orgasm. That kind of language makes it sound as if you are forcing someone to do something. Nothing about sex should be about force. It's a true shame that some people are hung up on squirting because they see it as a physical sign that they are a skilled lover.

The Practice

Okay. So, if you do want to explore whether you might be a squirter, take heed of the G-Zone exploration technique mentioned previously, paying particular attention to step 11—letting go and trusting your partner— because that is what tends to allow women to squirt.

Some people suggest that adding fisting to the sex menu can also lead to squirting. It's not the only way. But it does make sense, since fisting entails a great deal of ongoing G-Zone stimulation. And just so you know, fisting's central purpose is not to make a woman squirt. It's to give her pleasure. So it's a fun technique to explore whether or not squirting is of any interest or concern to you.

If you are on the receiving end of fisting, it is imperative that you feel safe, comfortable, and completely relaxed. Being fisted requires being fully open vaginally. For some women this state comes right after orgasm, and for others, right before. When you masturbate, pay attention to how your body opens and closes around orgasm to determine what stage might be the most comfortable for you.

Then have your partner follow these steps.

1. Use plenty of lube. Cover your entire hand and wrist, regardless of how wet your partner is. Lube is key.

2. Finger her first with one finger, then move up to two and then three, paying close attention to how her body responds. Check in with her to be sure she isn't experiencing any pain. Fisting should not hurt. It may cause her to feel pressure. But it shouldn't actually be uncomfortable or painful.

3. Fold your hand into itself, tucking your thumb inside, trying to make it as narrow and compact as possible.

4. Once you enter her up to where your hand is at its widest, it's time to take things slow. Very, very slow. Enter her the tiniest bit at a time, adding more lube and checking in with her as you go. Remind her to breathe and relax. Continue to look at her. Place your other hand between her breasts to ground her. You may have to rotate ever so slightly to get completely inside, and you may experience a sort of "sucking in" as her pussy takes in all of your hand.

5. Once inside of her, make a fist and then allow her to adjust to having your fist inside her. Talk to her. Check in with her. Remind her to breathe, and then, when she says she's ready, move to the next step.

6. Move very slowly and gently inside of her, trying both tiny rotations and tiny thrusts, until you discover just what she likes. If she is open enough, you may be able to draw your hand completely in and out and in and out and over again. You may want to combine fisting with clit stim, anal play, and/or breast play.

7. When she comes, allow her to ride the sensations for as long as she likes. This is when she may squirt. If she

doesn't, don't take it personally, and reassure her that it's not a problem should she feel disappointed. This is not a performance. It's an experience. There is no right or wrong way to have it.

8. When she is ready for you to withdraw, exit as gently as you entered.

9. Be sure to spend some time connecting after the experience. Even after the two of you have experienced this a number of times, it can still be an overwhelming connection that requires some emotional closure afterwards. Placing one hand over her entire vulva and one hand on her chest while maintaining steady eye contact is a great way to do this.

Here's how some women describe the sensation:

It feels empowering as opposed to relaxing.

It feels like a pleasure built up inside me is getting released and it spreads through my whole entire body.

It felt as though I was orgasming out rather than in.

Liberating, relaxing, rejuvenation of my whole body and mind, I feel like a new person. It's as if I have been holding all the tension in my body and at once releasing it all.

It was something that was unexpected and the ultimate high. I wasn't sure how to take it the first time, but I crave it!

It felt AMAZING. It is just a really intense orgasm. And on a deeper level it felt powerful as a woman to ejaculate, like I was taking on a more dominating role, especially ejaculating on my partner. Which I'm sure has to do with the feelings of traditional gender roles I was raised with in regards to sex and what I saw in porn at a younger age. Also playing into that, there is a real sense of pride when I ejaculate, like I've performed for my partner, showcasing how much they turned me on. I feel like they are proud of themselves and me so it is just a very high self-esteem experience.

Dear God, YES and YES!!!! Wow...how to describe this.... The most overwhelming feeling of love for someone after I came. The orgasm itself was soooo different from the others. Both times it happened, I used a toy on myself while being verbally guided by my girl over the phone. I could feel the pressure building—like you have to urinate. Mentally, I had to calm my mind and allow my body to release it. You just get lost in the deep pounding penetration (and afterwards you feel like you've broken your cervix!). But when I came, there wasn't the normal body-shaking explosion—it was just a sweet release...the sweetest release you could ever feel. The first time I soaked the bed. The second time—about a month later—I didn't soak it as much, but then again, it wasn't as slow, deep, and long as the previous time. But with this orgasm it's more about the aftereffects. Words will not ever truly give the feeling justice. I cried my first time. Why? Because I loved her. I loved her so much but we weren't at the point in our relationship where "I love you"s were being exchanged. All I wanted to do was tell her I loved her. The second time...she made me go look at myself in the mirror afterward because she thought I was the most beautiful thing she'd ever seen.

Ejaculation and squirting are neither required nor necessarily attainable by all women. They are not something you need to worry yourself over. Seriously. And if anyone is giving you a hard time or pressuring you, talk to them about how that makes you feel. If they can't understand, you need to ditch them.

Adding G-Zone involvement to your play, on the other hand, is a very attainable and reasonable goal if you are game. It involves some searching and some finesse. It involves the right tools, an interested partner, and an engaged mind. But if you are up for the exploration, it promises to be a fun one, and the results will be well worth the journey.

Once again, these are just tools and ideas and ways to play to add to your ultimate orgasm toolbox. So feel free to use and ignore at will. What I hope is that you won't feel pressure to do any of these things, just like you won't feel any pressure or shame that keeps you from doing them. There's no belt system or ranking in sex, just a wealth of opportunities to find your ultimate orgasm.

9

Going Deeper:
The A-Zone, the U-Zone,
Anal Play, and Multiple Orgasm

I HESITATED WHEN I titled this chapter, because I don't want you to think that there are beginner or "shallow" orgasms or that there is some kind of judgment around where you fall. That is simply not the case.

So these are "deeper" only in that they exist beyond already perfectly amazing orgasms, should you want to explore. They are not necessarily better. But they are, in some cases, quite different.

First, allow me to clarify. The A-Zone and the U-Zone are areas of the female body. They are places from which an orgasm can emanate. I want to emphasize that the physiological response that we call orgasm is one nerve response. One. What triggers that response can vary greatly, and can include the A-Zone and the U-Zone.

The same goes for anal play. It is an excellent addition to other activities in pursuit of the beloved orgasm of all orgasms—the blended orgasm.

The A-Zone
The Scoop
The A-Zone (aka the AFE zone, the anterior fornix erogenous zone, or the deep zone) is located between the cervix and the bladder. If this were the SAT, the explanation would go a little something like this: The

clitoris is to the penis as the A-Zone is to the prostate.

Women say that if the zone gets treated just right, the result can be downright mind-blowing. The best part is that the A-Zone is happy to serve again and again. Unlike the clit, it gets neither over-sensitized nor desensitized from being stimulated to orgasm.

In terms of the vaginal canal, the A-Zone is basically the ends of the earth. Because the cervix protrudes, ever so slightly, into the vagina, a circular recess is created all around it. The part of this recess that lies toward the front of the body is the anterior fornix. This grouping of nerves sits about two inches past the G-Zone and is much larger than its G-sister. Think of it as the messenger. Kick that zone into gear and it will let your brain and the rest of your body know that it is ready to play.

Many women, even those for whom other sexual activities don't have much effect, find that A-Zone stimulation can make them very wet and more responsive to whatever play may follow. It is also prone to downright violent contractions that feel insanely good. You can trust me on that.

The Practice

In order to stimulate the A-Zone, have your partner slide two fingers inside you. The middle and index finger are best. Reach in as far as you can go and you'll hit the magic spot.

You can also find A-Zone-specific toys that are long and thin with an upward curve at the end in order to reach this zone. Lelo's Elise 2 is one great option, and Dodson's Vaginal Barbell does the trick, too, if you prefer something sans vibration (it can also stay in place hands-free).

Speaking of toys, there is no shame in adding in some playful equipment. You know that old saying, "The right tool for the right job"? That's just as important in sex as it is in carpentry. You may miss out on some pretty knock-out orgasms if you aren't willing to invite the right tools into your bedroom. You don't want to become dependent on any one thing, of course. You want your body to be open and free enough to orgasm based on any number of sensations created by any number of body parts or toys.

Finding your ultimate orgasm is all about being open to exploration. The A-Zone definitely requires patience and an open mind if you are to benefit from what it offers.

Here's how to give it a whirl:

1. Lie on your back with your knees bent and your legs falling open to either side.
2. Have your partner massage your outer lips and, when you're ready, stimulate your clit manually, orally, and/or with a vibrator.
3. When your body is open and receptive (you'll know because you'll be very wet and wanting to be entered), have your partner slide her/his fingers inside you, curved upwards as far as she/he can reach. The end of the road is your A-Zone. Add lube if you experience any discomfort.
4. Have your partner try different strokes, pressures, and speeds to see what kicks your A-Zone into gear. Once you find the zone, consider making the A-Zone part of your combo play. Think A-Zone, clit, and anus, and you may just end up seeing stars.

It is important to keep in mind that this is not part of basic play. As Betty Dodson explained during an email conversation on July 22, 2014, "The more elusive deep vaginal thrusting that stimulates the base of the spine, now called the 'deep spot' requires an eight-inch penis or a quality silicone dildo." Fingers, of course, as I explain above, are an excellent alternative as well.

Not all women dig having their A-Zone stimulated. It's a very big feeling, and it may not be one you find pleasurable. But don't be scared off, either. Like many of the ideas and activities in this book, this might not be your deal right away. But it may become a favorite later on. Finding your ultimate orgasm takes time, an open mind, and, yes, an open pussy!

The U-Zone
The Scoop

It's strange to think there's a spot on women's bodies that was only recently "discovered." I mean, it's not like there hasn't been plenty of opportunity to explore them. Somehow, though, until quite recently, the U-Zone was not on anyone's radar. And even now that it is starting to show up on some sexuality charts and graphs, it is still quite the mystery.

But there's really no reason for the U-Zone to remain shrouded in secrecy. It's actually quite easy to find and quite fun to play with. The U-Zone is made up of hypersensitive, ridged tissues that can be found above and to either side of the urethral opening. It's super sensitive. The cool thing is, the more aroused it becomes, the more sensitive it becomes. It's like the good kind of self-fulfilling prophecy!

According to my email discussion with Garcia on October 19, 2014, the urethra is surrounded by erectile tissue (characterized by its spongy feel), which means that when it becomes sexually aroused, it fills with blood. But here's the really interesting part. This tissue is not just in this one spot. It goes from the anterior wall of the vagina, all around the urethra, and right on up to the pubic bone.

Pleasure travels. So that means that exciting any of these areas of tissue has the potential to ignite all these areas of tissue. In other words, let the party begin.

This is the tissue we talked about earlier, in the discussion about female ejaculation and squirting. This tissue is what has come to be known as the Skene's or periurethral glands or—ready for this?—the female prostate, and thus the source of female ejaculate.

The Practice

The U-Zone can be stimulated with your fingers or your tongue. To find it, look for the tiny hole above the vaginal opening. That's the urethra. The U-Zone is above and to either side of that opening. It's that easy, and it's incredibly sensitive. (Think the clit after it's already hard and ready to rumble.) So only the lightest pressure is required. Slide your

NICE TO KNOW U

Here's some more information from Dr. Madeleine Castellanos, a board-certified psychiatrist specializing in the treatment of sexual dysfunction and the improvement of sex life for couples or individuals, who wrote a piece on the U-spot (or U-Zone, as I prefer to call it) that includes this advice.

The U-spot feels the best when it is wet and touched gently. You do not need to put a lot of pressure on it, and many women have discovered this spot just from their partner rubbing the head of their penis up and down their labia. This is a motion that can be incorporated with stimulation of the clitoris and can be a way to reach orgasm all on its own for some women. The U-spot can also be stimulated with fingers, but remember—gentle stroking across it is usually more pleasurable than pushing on it (it's a spot, not a button). Once again, incorporating this stroking with stroking of the clitoris above it may also be a pathway to orgasm for some women. And as with all things having to do with sexuality and anatomy, some women have very sensitive U-spots, while some do not. When using fingers, you may find she likes to have some wet stroking all the way from the clitoris, over the U-spot and then just into the opening of the vagina. (Castellanos 2010) fingers across the U-Zone, alternating between vertically and horizontally. Making small circles around the spot can also do the trick. Try alternating between clockwise and counterclockwise to keep the pressure to a minimum.

Lubrication is key for U-Zone play, so be sure she is good and wet. The better the glide, the better the chance of orgasm. Very little pressure is needed, and please, no pushing. It's not the "easy" button. Simply running one's fingers or a toy up and down over it, combined with clit stim, has been known to send a girl to the outer limits of the stars. Whether you use a vibe or your fingers, the same caveats apply. Use lube. Be gentle.

Regardless of how you stimulate the U-Zone, it can definitely lead to orgasm euphoria. (However, beware of actually probing the opening, as that can lead to a UTI.)

When it comes to your tongue, you may have already ventured to the U-Zone without even realizing that this was a spot to be reckoned with. Some argue that the tongue is the best U-Zone tool in your arsenal, since when it comes to the U-Zone, the wetter (and the less chance for agitation) the better. In order to focus your efforts, do your best to locate the spot with your fingers first before setting your tongue to task.

Here's a great way to play with the U-Zone orally.

1. Have your partner place his or her tongue at the opening of your vagina.
2. Using a flattened tongue, have him or her lick upward to your clit. Think of peach juices dripping down your arm that you're trying to collect.
3. Have your partner play with pressure, speed, and exact location to find the best way to maximize the U-Zone!

Think of the U-Zone as another great addition to your menu of options. Have your partner explore it in combination with the other zones discussed in the book and you are sure to find your own magic combo.

But this is a good time to mention a really important aspect of any exploration of our own ultimate orgasm. It's a quote so classic as to have become a cliché, but it certainly rings true when it comes to orgasm exploration. "Life is a journey, not a destination," Ralph Waldo Emerson once said.

Orgasm, too, is not a destination; it's a journey. Once we begin to treat it and look at it as such, we will have much stronger, higher quality, and more frequent orgasms. We have gotten so focused on the endgame, we have totally lost track of the real fun, the actual play. The "Do you like this? How does that feel? Do you want more? What about this at the same time?" journey that makes sex the fun, intimate, engaging, and magnetic activity that it can be.

THE TONGUE AND U

Again from Dr. Castellanos:

[M]ost people would agree that oral sex is one of the best ways to stimulate the U-spot. This is because it already makes the area wet and has less friction than the skin of the fingers. The easiest way to find it is to find the opening of the vagina with your tongue, then softly and slowly lick upwards towards the clitoris, as if you are licking an ice-cream cone. This way, you can see which area she is most sensitive in, and you won't overwhelm her with too much pressure or speed. Once you find the spot she likes, you can experiment with putting different amounts of pressure with your tongue, or going faster or slower. (Castellanos 2010)

The Anal Zone
The Scoop

This can be a delicate subject. People often have very strong feelings about anal play. But it has the potential to be a major pleasure center if you are willing to take what might be a considerable leap, depending on your feelings on the subject.

As Betty Dodson explained via email July 22, 2014, "The anus has an abundance of sensitive nerve endings that can be utilized to enhance masturbation or partner sex. Penetrating the anus during partner sex is a more advanced form of sex and the people involved have to have sufficient information on how to proceed. A well-oiled finger during oral sex or vaginal penetration can be a welcome addition."

I know that some women object to anal play because it seems too naughty or too dirty (actually dirty, as in germs), but it's worth experimenting with. In combination with other activities, it can lead to a downright mind-boggling orgasm. Tidy up before you play and remind your partner not to put anything that has been in your ass anywhere else in or on your body afterwards.

Anal play was a tough one for me because I had to keep telling my mind that there was nothing wrong with it. Having your partner rub or gently enter you anally while rubbing or licking your clit and/or penetrating you vaginally will likely cause the kind of orgasm that requires a recovery period before you are capable of walking in a straight line again. So it's worth it to tell your brain to relax and allow your body to enjoy.

You shouldn't be afraid to enjoy the things that feel good to you, even those things that you never imagined liking. Schell (2011, 141) explains, "Many women are astonished to discover that they prefer anal to vaginal penetration. The deeply felt, unique sensations can lead a woman to know unprecedented sexual pleasure."

Forgive me for the body-positive pep talk I'm about to give you; I know it's not the first one you've gotten between these pages. But your body is amazing and it belongs to you and it has a right to pleasure and it has a right to have the kind of pleasure in the kind of ways that it naturally desires. Any pushback you're getting from your head is just social programming. It is your responsibility to ignore the negative messages that were designed to keep women contained and manageable.

Women are brilliant, orgasmic, complicated, juicy, dirty, desirable, and desirous creatures. Anyone who suggests anything less is out to control you or is filled with his or her own self-loathing that demands putting others down in order to raise him or herself up.

The bottom line is, anal play feels good. When I asked in my survey what women wanted to know about orgasm, a number of survey takers asked why exactly anal sex feels so good. Well, my first thought is, "Who cares. It just does. So don't fight it. Enjoy it!" But I'm guessing, dear reader, that you are hoping for more of a biological explanation. So I turned to Dr. Ellington via email August 12, 2014 (who is, as you might remember, an internationally recognized scientist in the area of sexual medicine) to address this:

> *Because of the size of the clitoris lying along the entire perineum, any pushing, pulling, or pressure in this area will stimulate arousal tissue and feel good. It is impossible to have any penile contact "down there" without stimulating the large arousal complex of women. Additionally, the rectum and anus itself also are highly sensitive. Many women enjoy rimming and finger or toy stimulation also for the same reason. The nerves to the perineal area are bundled with nerves to the clitoris. Stimulation of both areas causes increased arousal.*

The Practice

Here are some tips for how to get started with anal play.

1. Lube. No lube, no anal play. That is my number-one rule. Unlike the vagina, the anus is not self-lubricating. So get the good stuff and use it generously.
2. No pain required. Or desired. If there is pain (and not the likable kind), you may need more lube, a smaller insertion

object (finger or toy), or a slower, more gentle touch. If it hurts, say so and adjust accordingly.

3. Enter cautiously. There is nothing hot about your partner ramming something into your ass willy nilly. Have your partner take it slow and ask you how you're feeling. Half the fun is wanting more and having your partner tease you and ask for it rather than simply ramrodding you.

4. Keep it gentle—unless otherwise directed. Once she or he is in there, it's not a free-for-all, all bets are off situation. A slow and steady, in and out movement will likely be the most pleasurable. But, again, tell your partner what you want and need. Now is not the time to be shy.

5. Anal play is best as part of a blended orgasm. Some women may like anal play without any other action going on. But that is unusual at best. Some women like a finger in their ass and others just like the entrance played with. Regardless, most women enjoy it most when it is part of other activities involving the clit and/or the vagina.

6. Don't be scared off if at first you don't succeed. You might not get it right the first time. It might feel too foreign. It might hurt. It might be too scary. It might even make you cry. But it's new. And it's okay. So don't be afraid to take some time off and revisit it another time when you feel ready.

7. Anal play is by no means required. Many women find it to be the zenith, the final piece of the puzzle, the done and done in pursuit of the ultimate orgasm. But other women have virtually no need or desire for it. So you can take it or leave it. Just be sure that if you're leaving it, it's because you are truly not interested as opposed to just scared off by shame or society's bad habit of dictating what is "right" and "wrong" for women when it comes to sex.

8. Waxing is optional. Some women feel like there's no place for anal play if they aren't waxed. But that's really just about

how you feel comfortable. I personally like everything as smooth as can be. But there are women who prefer to keep things *au naturel,* and that is certainly their prerogative. It's all about doing what makes you feel sexy!

9. Try toys. Anal beads and butt plugs can be a fun way to dabble in anal play. They provide a variety of sensations and can help ease the weirdness factor if the idea of your partner's finger inside you makes you a little queasy at first blush. Plus, toys can stay inside your behind while your partner's hands are busy doing other things. Hands-free is a happy thing.

In speaking to Jude Schell about anal sex, I found this comment she made particularly interesting: "A lot of stock is put into the value of having a nice ass, yet that same perky posterior is all too frequently overlooked when prioritizing erogenous zones. Bottoms can be licked and kissed, massaged, stroked, lightly bitten, squeezed, spanked, and penetrated."

Women's asses are praised constantly. But it's true—when it comes to the bedroom, they are too oft ignored, often because of highly outdated taboos. Although interestingly enough, it is the taboo itself that can make the act of ass play all the more exciting. As Schell (2011, 87) explains, "A bond is created when lovers share the thrill of a traditionally taboo act. Even when not entering her, a significant degree of trust must exist to allow you to stimulate and explore her delicate, highly erogenous *tail zone.*"

While we're on the subject of backsides, don't forget about the power of the perineum. The perineum is diamond-shaped and very soft prior to arousal. It's located between the vaginal opening and the anus. Pressing against it activates a variety of erectile tissue nestled inside you, and it can make an orgasm go from nice to earth-shattering.

It wasn't until sex with a relatively recent partner that I learned how much perineum play is a part of my greatest pleasure. Whenever she would enter me, if she used downward pressure, it increased my orgasm exponentially. That came as a massive surprise to me, because that had just never really been a part of my sexual play.

Then, after meeting Betty Dodson and being aware of how it felt to have her fist against my perineum when I orgasmed, I realized what a standard go-to this should probably be. She focused right in on that spot as soon as I was having trouble peaking, and then—bang!—I came.

Have your partner explore your perineum both by using downward pressure when entering you and by using external pressure manually. I would be very surprised if it didn't in some way raise your orgasm quotient.

And just like with anything new, slow and steady wins the race. Never is that more apropos than when it comes to anal play.

The Multiple Orgasm
The Scoop

Ah, the multiple orgasm. It's a thing of beauty. And a thing of reality. So let's start there. Women do have multiple orgasms. We are very lucky in that respect. Women do not have a refractory period—or downtime—like men do. Once we're up, we have every opportunity to go up and up and up!

So, how exactly does one manage this feat? Follow your body's lead. When you have an orgasm, either ease up on or stop what you were doing. But don't stop your brain. Allow it to continue thinking about what you just did, how good it felt, and what might feel good next. Then slowly ease back in or start again (depending on whether or not you came to a complete halt).

The biggest holdup when it comes to multiple orgasms is what I call the "greedy girl" factor. Girls are raised to be polite and restrained. They are supposed to ask before they take a cookie. Wait for everyone else at the table to be served. Accept whatever size serving they receive and not ask for seconds—because that's only for greedy girls.

Sure, polite is great. I am all about being civilized. I demand it, actually. Everywhere except in bed, that is. When it comes to sex,

THREE CHEERS FOR THE BACK DOOR

I love this piece from Tristan Taormino about anal play. If you have any doubts about why people dig it, this should quell them.

Yes, I admit it—I love anal sex. The first time someone put a finger in my butt, I thought I'd died and gone to heaven. I think I almost went crazy from the pleasure. The sensations I experienced were so intense that I felt high from the experience, and I couldn't wait to do it again. The first time I put my finger in someone else's butt, the results were just as fabulous—I felt entrusted with my partner's deepest deepest vulnerabilities, in awe of the ecstatic pleasure I could give. Then came more fingers, tongues, vibrators, small dildos, bigger dildos, butt plugs, cocks, bigger butt plugs, even an entire small hand. Each time I could take a little more and give a little more, I felt more sexually alive and powerful. As I incorporated anal eroticism into my sex life, my sex life became better and better. The sex got hotter, my partners more adventurous, my orgasms fierce and explosive. The physical sensations were undeniably some of the best I'd ever felt in my life. I confess too that beyond the deep body gratification, the naughtiness of it all really turned me on. (Taormino 2006, xi) unrestrained is the only way to go. I'm not saying to forgo the "please" and "thank you." But I am definitely saying that you leave "I don't want to come across as the greedy girl" behind.

Ask for what you want. Enjoy it when you get it. Ask for more when you've already had some. Believe me, a good partner will dig it. In fact, a good partner will absolutely love it. There is nothing sexier than a woman who wants to simply get lost and enjoy.

There is no reason not to enjoy every last drop of pleasure that your body is willing to savor. A good partner will be flattered and thrilled that you want more. So turn off that part of your brain that's telling you one orgasm is plenty and listen instead to your body which is likely saying, "Shall we have another go?"

The Practice

Here are a few tips for upping the multiple orgasm ante:

1. Don't think about it. I know, I know. It's impossible not to. But you're just going to have to do your best. Performance anxiety is one of the most powerful killers of great orgasms—particularly multiple ones. Don't get caught in a negative loop: "I'm never going to come" or "I'm never going to be able to get there again" or "I want to keep going, but hasn't it already taken me long enough? How can I ask for more?"

2. The best way to quiet a negative loop is to replace it with a positive one. Something along the lines of "That feels really good." "I love it when my partner touches me like that." "I feel so sexy." "I look so sexy."

3. Better yet, talk to your partner. Tell your partner what you are experiencing and what you want and what you like and how amazing she/he is. A little flattery goes a long way—especially in bed. If you like what's happening, why keep that information to yourself? There is nothing

MULTIPLE MADNESS

I love these wise words on multiple orgasm from Felice Newman in her book *The Whole Lesbian Sex Book*.

Women can and do have multiple orgasms. Which doesn't mean you should have multiple orgasms or even that multiple orgasms are more satisfying than ordinary single orgasms.... But many women do find that one orgasm leads to another, with very little time lapse in between.... Rather than relaxing into afterglow, these women go right back to the plateau stage and come over and over. Some women experience this as a series of smaller orgasms; others experience orgasms that increase in intensity and duration, leading up to a really big bang.... How do you achieve multiple orgasms? In The Good Vibrations Guide to Sex, *Cathy Winks and [Anne] Semans offer three rules for achieving multiple orgasms: "back off, breathe, and move." After you come, and your clit is too sensitive to touch, back off without entirely ceasing stimulation. Winks and Semans suggest switching to a lighter or less direct touch. Then breathe. Breathing oxygenates your body and keeps the energy flowing. And move—move your pelvis, your legs, your feet. (Newman 1999, 52)* that inspires a lover more and makes her or him want to keep you coming and coming than hearing how great she or he is!

4. Mix it up. Often, having multiple orgasms is about doing something at least a little different from what just made you come. So if oral sex was what sent you over the edge, have your partner penetrate you while stimulating your clit orally or manually or with a toy. For round three, try a little anal play. And since the clit is the primary orgasm go-to, there's no reason to ignore it during any round. But it can be fun and effective to play with blending different elements. By the time you're done, you really will be truly spent.

5. Talk dirty. To stay focused, say the words and ask your partner to get in on the game. Talking about what is happening can be very hot. "You make me so wet." "I'm going to come for you." "I love being your naughty girl." Whatever fits your dirty-talk genre. Or engage in a little fantasy. Entice your partner to spin a naughty story for you that incorporates the things that she knows turn you on, like that pretty hotel clerk or a new toy or a public place where you've always wanted to have sex. It doesn't have to be complicated. All it has to do is turn you on and keep you focused on pleasure.

6. Stay with it. The ultimate key to multiple orgasms is staying with it for as long as it feels good and not stopping because you're worried about the time or the laundry or your thighs or someone else's orgasm. Don't forget, we are each responsible for our own orgasms. So have as many as you like. This isn't cookies at Sunday school. There are plenty to go around, and you can do as much touching and taking as you please.

Consider these more tools to add to your toolbox. You don't have to have them. But they sure are fun to have. There is nothing more empowering than listening to your desires and sharing them with someone who gets you and who is as committed as you are to finding your ultimate orgasm.

Mysterious Orgasms:
Breasts, Mouth, and Skin

I CALL THIS THE "Mysterious" section because these are the orgasms you hear tell of at cocktail parties and wonder, "Really? Can all women do that, or is she just some sort of nympho or liar or show-off?" Well, no, no, and maybe.

As I've said before and I'm sure to say again, when it comes to sexuality, almost anything is possible. Can women come from just breast, mouth, or skin stimulation? Sure. Is it common? Are these things we all need to work toward? Not at all and only if you want to. But they can sure be fun to explore, and there's no harm in such exploration, unless you fall into that danger zone of thinking it's some sort of failure if you don't come.

Breasts
The Scoop

Breasts are a puzzler. For some women, they are erotic hot spots that can drive them to orgasm. For other women, stimulating them can be a nice accompaniment, but far from a main attraction. And for others, they can actually be more of an annoyance than a turn-on when stimulated.

So, first things first: As with all your other equipment, be honest about how yours work and how you like them operated. And if you think it may have been operator error in the past that caused them to be a nonstarter, be sure to share that with your partner, too. Who knows? Maybe this person knows how to get you buzzing from a place others have missed out on.

Having your breasts touched can be a nice sensation in general. But it's the nipples that play the primary role if we're talking about orgasm. Betty Dodson explained in her July 22, 2014 email, "It has been shown that some women have very sensitive nipples that can lead to an orgasm. Usually nipple play is only part of a woman's arousal mechanism."

The science behind this is relatively simple. Stimulating a woman's nipples causes them to become erect as they fill with blood. The brain quickly gets the memo from the nipples. Something along the lines of, "Damn, that feels good. Maybe an orgasm is in order?" Oxytocin, known as the "feel-good" hormone, is also released during nipple play. And oxytocin, of course, triggers orgasm.

So that leaves us with the big question. Can a woman actually come from having her breasts stimulated? Or perhaps, more specifically, from having her nipples sucked? Well, all I can tell you is that women do report that they have had orgasms from that with nothing else going on. No other rubbing or touching or penetration. Nothing. But it's not common, I can assure you of that.

How is that possible? Well, there is MRI-based research that proves that stimulating the nipples engages what is known as the *genital sensory cortex* in the brain, which, you guessed it, is the same spot that gets all abuzz from clitoral, vaginal, and cervical (A-Zone) stimulation. Not to mention that breasts can swell up to 25 percent when stimulated.

Jude Schell (2005, 53) explains, "Stimulating these nerve endings incites tingling and increases her receptivity. Like the clitoris, vaginal, and anal regions, a stimulated nipple fills with blood, swells, and becomes erect, rendering it and the area around the nipple particularly receptive to any extra attention."

So there's enough scientific evidence to make orgasms that emanate from the breasts at least worth exploring. I just wouldn't want you to judge yourself or your partner based on whether or not you can wrangle this feat, because it's definitely not common, nor is it in the top three reported types when it comes to powerful orgasms. (Those would be clitoral, anal, and blended by my counts, in case you were wondering.)

The Practice

As for the how-to, that can run the gamut, from gentle pulling and tugging to more aggressive pinching and biting and even slapping. (Don't be shocked. Some girls go crazy for that.) Sucking is perhaps the most effective method for arousal. Have your partner massage both breasts in her hands while sucking, gently at first and then more strongly, on one nipple and then the other.

In general, though, most women don't care for the "radio dial" handling of nipples that some men seem prone to. So feel free to tell any partner—nicely, of course—that that's not what those things are there for.

More common than a nipple-*only* orgasm is the chance that, as Betty mentions, you might find breast or nipple play a welcome addition to other sexual activities. It's all about creating the perfect combo.

If you want to give it a go, here are some steps to help you get there.

1. As with most sexual play, it's ideal to start out with some old-school making out. You cannot underestimate the power of kissing. It is oft overlooked and really should not be.

2. Have your partner kiss and lick and suck and bite his or her way down from your mouth to your neck to your ears to your breasts. This is not the time for rushing. This is the time for lingering.

3. Now it's time to move to the main event. Have your partner kiss and rub and lick your breasts, using lapping motions with the tongue while following closely behind with gentle fingertip touches. Although you will likely be

itching for him or her to get to your nipples, be patient. The more time it takes, the better it will be when she gets to the goodies.

4. Here's my favorite part. Now's it's time for your partner to tease each nipple as if it were your clit. Have your partner tend to one breast at a time, holding it and then gently pinching the nipple and pulling it lightly taut. Then have your partner suck and bite and lick and flick your nipple the same way he or she would your clit during oral sex. Have your partner draw circles around it with his or her tongue. You can even have him or her give them a "blow job" of sorts, if you can imagine the nipple as a tiny penis. This works better on more prominent nipples, of course. Allow your partner to play and explore and dine on you with no goal in mind beyond your pleasure, switching sides and going back and forth between the two as he or she pleases—and as it pleases you.

Note: Keep in mind that time of month, body modifications (like piercings), arousal, and whether or not you have just come (or are just about to come) can greatly affect sensitivity.

Whether or not this brings you to orgasm makes no difference. Regardless, it is likely to leave you very much in the mood for more sexual play. If it does lead to orgasm, you are in for an oxytocin treat, as breast orgasms make for quite the oxytocin release. As you may recall, oxytocin is the lovely, lovey-dovey happy drug known for making you feel happy and snuggly and very bonded to the person who caused the release.

And remember that the breasts can be an excellent part of combo play. I love this tip from Schell: "Lightly yet firmly tweak or bite down on her nipple just as she's climaxing, a move that requires exquisite timing, yet often results in an especially sweet orgasm" (*The Guide to Lesbian Sex*, 55).

Finding your ultimate orgasm involves playing with every angle. So when you feel comfortable, invite your partner to add new layers to your sexual play and to experiment with timing and pressure and speed and locations of touch.

Mouth
The Scoop

Our mouths are amazing. When it comes to sex, we can use them to kiss and suck and bite and lick. And because they are a wet opening, it's hard not to transfer the sensations one feels in one's mouth to the opening between your legs. In other words, if a partner runs her tongue all around your lips, you may feel yourself getting wet, imagining that tongue circling your other lips. If your partner sucks on your upper lip, you may well feel your clit swelling and responding, imaging itself as the object of that attention.

Women have reported coming from kissing or having their lips licked and sucked or even from licking and sucking a partner's fingers. The bottom line is this: Never underestimate the power of the mind.

The Practice

If you want to give it a whirl, take some time to enjoy an old school make-out session like you did as a teenager. Think about nothing but how your partner tastes and how his or her mouth feels on yours. Imagine it's your pussy and not your mouth being savored so meticulously. Give in to sounds you might find yourself wanting to make. And don't be tempted to move on to other activities. See how long you can take the mouth feast and see if it can take you all the way.

The good news is, even if doesn't (which I personally would not count on), you will be incredibly aroused, and whatever you choose to move on to next is bound to be amazing.

On that note, this seems like a good time and place to talk about expectations. Having reasonable ones is incredibly important when it comes to orgasms. It is far better to feel like you're overachieving than to feel like you're underachieving.

Your expectation should be to have orgasms when you engage in activities that simulate your clit either directly or indirectly. I consider everything else frosting or gravy, depending on whether you're a sweet or salty girl!

I don't know if it's pornography or romantic comedies or folklore, but I believe we have come to have some very unhealthy expectations when it comes to orgasms. They don't happen quickly. They don't all last thirty minutes or make you pass out, although some of mine certainly do, with my new partner at least. And again, vaginal intercourse alone does not do it for the majority of women.

There are all sorts of party tricks. But nothing is like the meat and potatoes—slow penetration with clitoral stimulation and, if you're game, anal stimulation as well. Throw in breast stimulation and kissing, and you've got yourself a recipe for the kind of orgasm that we should all be more than happy to live with!

BREAST PLAY 101

I love Felice Newman's "How-To's of Breast Play" from *The Whole Lesbian Sex Book*. So I wanted to share her tips and tricks too!

- *Lick your partner's chest and underarm, working your way to her breasts.*
- *Experiment with a range of sensations from very light touches to very rough.*
- *Lick and nibble the sensitive underside of her breasts.*
- *Bury your face between her breasts.*
- *Cup the breasts in your hands, squeezing them together.*

- *Press her breast into your chest.*
- *Lick your fingers and swirl the wetness over her nipple. Or, use a drop of lube, edible flavored lotion, or even her own juices (if you don't intend to suck her nipple again or are fluid bonded).*
- *Stroke her nipple quickly and lightly, alternating with sharp pinches.*
- *Blow air on her moist nipple.*
- *Roll a nipple between your fingers. Lick and suck the tip as you would her clit.*
- *Squeeze her breasts together and lick both nipples simultaneously.*
- *Pinch and squeeze the nipples between thumb and forefinger.*
- *Grab a pair of nipple clamps to stimulate her breasts, leaving your hands free for other things.*
- *Rub your vulva over her breast; or rub your nipple on her clit after orgasm.*
- *Turn a blow job into breast play. "Tit fucking" needn't be reserved for heterosexual porn. After she's sucked your strap-on cock, slip your saliva-lubed cock between her breasts and thrust inside her cleavage. You can slide your cock back and forth between her breasts as she sucks.* (Newman 1999, 150–151).

MOUTH-TO-MOUTH

I love this kissing list from Violet Blue's book titled, but of course, *Kissing*. Here's what Blue says is on the menu for mouth-to-mouth play.

- *Nibble. Nibbles are little bites using only your lips, or your upper lip with your tongue.*
- *Graze. When you graze an area of [your partner's] body, you simply brush your lips over it.*
- *Trace. Similar in technique to grazing, tracing can be done in all the same ways but instead using the tip of your tongue.*
- *Breathe together. With both mouths open, nothing is sexier than inhaling someone's breath, literally taking [your partner's] breath away.*
- *Sweet kisses. These are light, full mouth kisses, but with no tongue.*
- *Speak. Whispering or speaking gently into your partner's open mouth between kisses is incredibly arousing.*
- *Lip presses. These are similar to sweet kisses above but without any movement, and more pressure.*
- *Bottom lip/top lip. This technique focuses your attention on [your partner's] top or bottom lip.*
- *Corners of the mouth. Don't neglect the corners of [your partner's] mouth when you're kissing.*
- *Open mouth. No tongue. A terrific transition technique that can be used over and over at every stage.* (Blue 2014, 65–69)

Skin

The Scoop

Skin is highly sensitive. More sensitive in some places than others, of course. But we generally don't give our skin enough credit when it comes to registering sensation. Some women say they can come from being stroked and massaged in places that are not necessarily considered erogenous zones.

As Betty Dodson explained in her July 22, 2014 email, "The entire body can be seen as an erogenous zone as long as nerve endings are functioning."

Skin also likes to be pulled, pinched, slapped, and bitten. If you find that you like a little pain, that's nothing to be worried about; lots of people do.

Unfortunately, many people still think of BDSM as something to be ashamed or frightened of. Unless, of course, you don't admit to liking it and you are whisked away by a rich man and you're really a very nice girl who would never do such a thing. Then it's okay. Argh.

Forget all that.

You may be a very nice girl *and* like a little BDSM (which is about Bondage, Discipline, Domination, Submission, Sadism, and Masochism. The acronym comes from all of those sort of squashed together). Talking about orgasms that emanate from our skin or our minds (which is next up) is a great place to talk about this, actually.

BDSM is about letting go and indulging in fantasies. It's about admitting what turns you on and not apologizing for your desires. Bondage is about being tied up or otherwise restrained, or tying up or restraining your partner. Discipline can be about spanking or flogging or otherwise punishing or being punished. Domination is about controlling someone or being controlled. Sadism is about deriving pleasure from causing someone else pain, and masochism is about deriving pleasure from your own pain, which brings up a very important topic: consent.

Sex is about two things: enthusiastic consent and pleasure.

Enthusiastic consent is sexy. And so are safe words. Once you have a partner's full consent and you have a safe word in place, you can do all the things that you desire, even the dark things.

That includes fantasies that might make you feel equal parts disturbed and turned on. Take, for example, the forceful submission fantasy conundrum. No woman wants to be raped. Under any circumstances. Ever. Rape is a crime of violence. It is a violation, a weak and unacceptable grasp at power.

A rape fantasy, or a forceful submission fantasy (the phrasing I greatly prefer), is about *choosing* to relinquish control to someone of your choosing.[4] It's about saying yes outside of the game and then letting the game begin, allowing you to play at being taken. The key word being *play.* So don't feel guilty for having rape fantasies, and partners, don't feel bad about fulfilling them if you feel comfortable doing that.

The key to acting out a great fantasy is the key to great sex—and relationships for that matter—communication. Spend an evening talking about your fantasies and how they look, who and what they include, and so on. Then talk about when you would be comfortable acting them out. Do you want it to be a surprise, or is that too scary? Nothing is wrong or off-limits. Let me say that again, because it might be one of the most important things you'll read in this book. Nothing is wrong or off-limits, as long as it's between enthusiastically consenting adults committing to one another's pleasure on equal ground without power imbalances or other mitigating factors.

I have toyed with some of my own forceful submission fantasies. I'll admit, it's something that intrigues me greatly and turns me on immensely. But I am also irrationally afraid that wanting it is somehow tempting fate and suggesting to the universe that I am welcoming sexual violence. Nothing could be further from the truth, of course. And I am working through that, especially with my current, new partner.

I imagine her telling me to turn around, get on my knees, and brace

---

4   See Pat Hawley's brilliant paper titled "Social Dominance and Forceful Submission Fantasies: Feminine Pathology of Power" in the *Journal of Sex Research* for more on this.

myself with my hands on the wall. My breath catching. My heart racing. I turn my head and look into her eyes and cannot possibly ignore the intensity staring back. I oblige and can immediately feel myself getting wetter as she pushes my legs open wider and runs her hand down my back forcefully. I am hers. But I am hers because I choose to be, and it is thrilling.

I also imagine making her expose herself in public and allow me to take her in front of strangers, despite her Southern distaste for PDA. Her tendency towards the conservative in "real life" tends to make her fantasy life veer towards all things "inappropriate," and her tendency for being in control and in charge in "real life" tends to make her taste in all things sexual more on the submissive side. Although she plays hard at dominant too. It's all about exploring the edges.

But I digress. The point of all of this is to say that your skin is a very sensitive thing, and although some women can come from the most unlikely bits of it being stimulated, even if all the skin attention doesn't cause an orgasm, it will likely cause a heck of a lot of arousal.

Keep in mind that some tucked away areas of skin that don't get exposed unless opened, like one's pussy or ass, may react quite happily just from being exposed. So invite your partner to open you like a present and you are both likely to get gifted. Sometimes the simple act of my girl spreading open my inner lips while she stimulates my clit can give me an orgasm of the rather insane variety.

The Practice

Treating every inch of your body as an erogenous zone can be a really fun thing to work toward. Have your partner start at the top of your head, massaging you and rubbing and teasing and touching you. Take note of what you're feeling and share with your partner as she/he goes. Have her/him stay where you find you are becoming more and more aroused and move on from where you are not.

Some places women find particularly sensitive are their scalps, necks, the insides of their elbows and knees, and their inner thighs. But you have the whole landscape to work with. So don't be shy and don't rush.

Keep in mind that it's not just the area of skin, but also how it's handled. For example, using a feather or flogger, or, if you want to get a little on the kinky side, try a Wartenberg wheel (sometimes called a Wartenberg Pinwheel). It was created by a man named Robert Wartenberg who was seeking a way to test nerve reactions. It is generally made of stainless steel and comprises a handle and a wheel with radiating, evenly shaped pins, which are rather sharp. The wheel rotates as the pins are rolled across the skin. Don't knock it till you try it, is all I'm going to say.

Here are a few more specific steps to set you on the right path.

1. Start with a steamy bath or shower. Water can have a powerful effect on the skin, waking it up and creating a variety of sensations.
2. Ask your partner to massage you with oil. Have him or her start at your scalp and move down to your toes. Focus on each body part as it is massaged. Pay attention to what feels good to you. Ask your partner to spend more time on those spots and try a variety of different techniques and pressure levels.
3. Engage your mind. As your partner touches you, imagine him or her touching you between your legs the same way he or she is stroking you elsewhere. The mind is a powerful instrument. See if you can get yourself to transfer each touch. Women have been known to come without a bit of contact with their naughty bits, just from the power of mentally transferring the touch from one body part to another.

Every part of the female body has the potential for inciting—and maybe even delivering—an orgasm. The most important thing to keep in mind is that there's no harm in trying.

An experiment that ends in failure is still a positive step in the right direction. It means that you are taking the risks and doing the things and

GET ROPED IN

As I mentioned, the skin can respond deliciously when presented with new and different textures and sensations. Rope play can be just the trick to exciting the skin—and the rest of you, for that matter. Tristan Taormino explains:

Rope is endlessly versatile, whether you can barely tie your shoelaces or you memorize the entire Ashley Book of Knots. Don't let yourself be intimidated by thinking that you have to know fancy knots. If you like complicated, that's great, but you don't need to know them.

Selecting the right material is key. Cotton rope is fantastic for beginners. Look for it in magic stores and better sex stores. Avoid nylon, polypropylene, and most other synthetics, as it's easy to cause rope burns with them. Hemp, jute, raw silk, and bamboo ropes are lovely, but they're quite expensive. When you're starting out, stick to shorter lengths of ten, fifteen, or twenty feet. Nothing kills a hot scene like the top getting tangled up in his or her own rope. (Taormino 2012, 103)

Check out Taormino's *The Ultimate Guide to Kink* for some beginner rope-tying techniques, including the single-column rope tie, the double-column rope tie, and open-leg crab variation.

opening the space for discovering just what will lead you to your ultimate orgasm. You may never know what your breasts or your mouth or your skin can do for your orgasmic life if you don't give them a chance at bat. And with the right partner, there are no real risks.

So what if all you end up with is a great massage or a killer make-out session or some very well-tended-to breasts? Even if these things don't turn you on sexually, they will still very likely wake you up sensually, and when it comes to orgasm, that is at least half the battle.

The clitoris is the center of female orgasm. But that doesn't mean that you have to focus on it to the exclusion of all other body parts. It just means that it is likely your key player, your lead actress, your main course. But no team or cast or meal is ever as good without its outfield, its chorus, or its side dishes.

Amazing orgasms are such a mind-bender because they require equal parts mindfulness and turning off your mind. They require equal parts tuning in and tuning out. They require focusing on a single thing and many things and nothing all at the same time.

It's a lot like cliff diving. You have to look out below and avoid the rocks and take the other people around you into consideration. But most importantly, above all else, you have to dive in.

Your Brain on Orgasm

The Mind-Body Connection
The Scoop

ONE SURVEY TAKER ASKED me how to keep the mind from dictating or limiting the pleasures of the body, which really got me thinking about just how integral the brain is in the search for the ultimate orgasm.

It's a big question and it deserves a big answer, because the brain and the orgasm are inseparable bedfellows. If you can't get the brain on board, getting the orgasm—a really good one, anyway—to follow is nearly impossible.

Getting your brain in the game is the hardest and easiest thing to do. It's the hardest because you have to tell your mind that there is nothing wrong with your sexual wants and needs, because there isn't (as long as it's with consenting adults, of course). It's the easiest because you are the boss of it. Completely. All you have to do is tell your brain where to be.

But the only way to do that is to, well, do it. Start by creating a sex-positive mantra for yourself. Something like "Sex is about pleasure and I deserve to feel pleasure," or "I have a right to have an orgasm the way I want to have an orgasm," or "There's nothing wrong with sex." Or whatever. The point is to have a positive tape to run through your mind to keep the negative one at bay.

Read sex-positive books. Watch sex-positive films. Surround yourself with sex-positive friends. Are you beginning to see a theme here? The point is that, if you feed your mind shame, then shame is what your brain will be occupied with. If you feed your mind positive messages about sex and desire and your body, then positive messages are what will follow.

The brain is the biggest sex organ you have. You need it in order to have the kind of earth-shattering orgasms that you have a right to. So you need your mind on board. It's not a quick or easy process. But it's worth it. You have to ban the negative and support the positive. You'll be amazed at just how much better sex gets when your mind allows your body to go where it longs to go.

The truth is that control can be a huge factor when it comes to orgasm, and that's not necessarily a bad thing. But if needing to be in control keeps you from having an orgasm, then letting go is imperative. That's usually about letting go of fear or shame. And that can be something you want to work on with a therapist if it has to do with trauma. Or you might just try the tips I mentioned above if it's more about the shame that society and religion and the like have a bad habit of instilling in many of us.

If your brain is the problem, here are a few tricks for getting your brain to play nicely:

1. Set the mood. Whatever that means to you. It can be hard to transition from the everyday to having a great orgasm. So set the lighting. Switch on the music. Reach for those candles. Whatever does it for you, whatever says to your brain, *It's time!*

2. Let go of the other thoughts taking up space in your head. The bills and your job and your needy BFF will all still be there later. Right now is about you and your orgasm. As thoughts pop into your brain, thank them for stopping by and send them on their way. I have a friend who says to

scoop them up, wrap them in love, and push them away.[5] I like that visual, and it gives my brain something to do while I'm trying to clear it.

3. Focus on where you're being touched. We've gotten too disembodied in this life. Too often, we actually miss out on the sensations our bodies are having. So when you touch yourself or are being touched by a partner, take notice of what your body is experiencing. This can help you to discover what you really do (and don't) like. And it can help with communicating those likes and dislikes with a partner. It's hard to ask for what you want when you don't know what you want.

4. Remind yourself to stay in the moment. If you start to drift, focus on your partner (or your own amazing self if you're masturbating) and remind yourself not to miss the wonderful thing that's going on right now while you're worrying about things that can most certainly wait— maybe forever!

You want your mind involved in sex. So it's not necessarily about fully letting go. You can be in control of your own orgasm. How it happens. When it happens. Who it happens with. But you want your mind to help you, not hinder you. So if needing to be in control means holding back, then relinquishing control is key. But if needing control is about guiding your orgasm or feeling in charge of your orgasm, then no worries, because you have every right to control your own pleasure.

All of this explains why fantasy so greatly impacts orgasms, sometimes even more than the actual connection that you might have with the person with whom you are playing.

Sex is about pleasure. It can also be about connection, and connection can be amazing. But first and foremost, sex is about pleasure. And fantasy

---

5   Thank you to Jimmy Belasco for this practice. (http://peacelovejimmy.wordpress.com)

feeds our ability to experience pleasure. So there's nothing wrong with imagining yourself a hero at the scene of a crime, a damsel in distress, a doctor administering a special exam, or a dignitary taking advantage of "political perks."

Whatever gets your brain off, will get your body off. The mind-body connection cannot be underestimated when it comes to sex. If you aren't having orgasms, or you aren't having the kinds of orgasms that you want to be having, and all your parts are working, your brain is a good place to check in with next. Ask yourself these questions:

1. When I'm having sex, am I thinking about sex or about things that turn me on?
2. When I want to or plan to or hope to have sex soon, do I think about sex or things that turn me on?
3. When I am having sex or thinking about sex, do feelings of shame or fear fill my head?

The truth is that a sexually healthy brain is as important as a sexually healthy body when it comes to having great orgasms. If the laundry is on your mind, how can you expect your body to respond? If your brain is telling you that there's something wrong with what your body is doing, how can you expect to come?

The Practice

Great orgasms are about giving in to sensation, and the only part of you that can do that is your brain. Allow it to slip away to the naughty side and you will be amazed at where your body can go. All you need is for your brain to sign off on the adventure.

Fantasy

If the idea of fantasizing seems daunting, that's perfectly understandable. Women are told that they're not supposed to have "dirty thoughts." But you're going to just have to let that idea go. Otherwise, you are going to miss out on a huge part of finding your ultimate orgasm.

Schell explains:

> *Role playing can release us of our inhibitions and nurture deeper feelings of trust and intimacy between lovers.... The best fantasy has a hint of possibility. This is true even if your fantasy is to do something you would never act out in reality. Beyond the sexual turn-on benefits of fantasizing are the additional and often surprising intellectual, emotional, and spiritual responses you can have as you discover and ponder a previously hidden or undeveloped side of yourself. The simple act of freeing your mind and allowing yourself to imagine that you are doing what you consider to be excitingly unusual or different stimulates your potential to enjoy sex more fully* (The Guide to Lesbian Sex, 129).

So, how do you fantasize? Let your mind wander. Think about what turns you on and let your brain follow that path as it chooses. That can be incredibly different for each person. Here are a few story starters to get you pointed in the right direction. But don't feel limited or put off by these. They may all interest you, or none of them may interest you. It doesn't really matter. All that matters is that you let your brain do as it pleases. And what the brain does best when it comes to fantasizing is to wander and play.

1. It wasn't how you expected the night to go. But now it seems as if there's no stopping it. The car pulls into the dark parking lot, and immediately X's mouth is on you. X's hands find their way to your hair and then make their way down your body. The rain pounds against the hood of the car and you feel lost as X pulls away sharply and without a word leaves you in the car. Alone. Your door opens, and X whisks you from the seat and pushes you hard against the hood. In seconds your pussy is exposed to

the cold and rain and you find yourself wanting X more than you've ever wanted anyone before...

2. The doorbell rings and for a moment you consider not even answering it. It's probably someone selling either magazines or religion, and you have no need for either. After the third ring you get up in a bit of a huff and make your way to the door. You look through the peephole and you can't believe who is there. You open the door slowly, knowing exactly what's about to happen and your lack of will or desire to stop it...

3. The campfire blazes in the dark night and you can't stop looking at X. The truth is, X can't stop looking at you either. It's been three days of this already and you're starting to go mad. You agreed to just be friends. It only makes sense. The age difference is nuts, right? What do you need with a forty-five year old? You're only twenty-five. You have nothing in common. X will get bored with you. You have no experience. You've never traveled or had a real job. And yet you always have such a good time together, and this trip...everyone is starting to notice. There's a pull between the two of you. So when X asks if you want to go for a walk by the river, you take a deep breath and say nothing more than *yes*...

Anyway, you get the idea. The point is, if you can dream it up, it's perfectly valid fodder for a fantasy, whether it's a doctor's office or a dungeon, a peer or a cougar, a stranger or a close friend. The point is, if it turns you on, have at it. Great fantasies lead to great orgasms.

Mindgasms
The Scoop

This is a tough one. There are women who say they can come with absolutely no physical stimulation. No sitting on the dryer. No practicing their Kegels. No squeezing their thighs together.

The mind is a powerful thing. So it makes sense that it can protect you in a dangerous situation, lead you to a solution in a perplexing situation, and bring you to an orgasm in a sexual situation—even if that situation is only in your mind.

I personally have not had an orgasm strictly from thinking about sexual scenarios. But there are certainly women who say they have. And as you probably know by this point in the book, I would never discount anyone's sexual experience.

The likelihood of having a mental orgasm is not particularly high. And the need for them probably isn't either. In fact, some women find themselves rather tormented by not being able to control these "mind-gasms." I mean, orgasms are great. But you don't necessarily want to have one while playing volleyball at the company picnic or eating turkey at the family Thanksgiving dinner.

Here's how two of the women I surveyed described a mental orgasm.

Woman One: With the mind it's kind of an out-of-body feeling. The way I try to explain it to others is that if someone has intense sexual energy and I walk into a room, I'm going to feel it. So I stay in a state of arousal. It can be very distracting at times, but most of the time it's very empowering for me.

Woman Two: Mine was from non-moving penetration with my partner speaking sexual words to me. That's it. No movement.

The Practice

If you do want to give mental orgasm a try, here are the steps to follow.

1. Put yourself in a safe, comfortable environment where you have the luxury of experiencing whatever this process might lead you to. It's possible that it could get highly emotional or lead you to wanting to masturbate. So it's ideal to be in a space where you can be totally relaxed and open to experiencing whatever might come.

2. Focus on your breathing. Think about each inhale and follow it through your body as it goes in your nose, through your lungs, and then down into your pelvis. Exhale slowly, focusing as you do. Tease yourself with that breath. Imagine it landing between your legs and then slowly slipping away.

3. Think dirty thoughts. Imagine the last time you had an amazing orgasm. Focus on your senses. What did you feel, hear, see, smell, and taste? Who was there? What happened? If you need a little inspiration, switch on some sex-positive, woman-positive porn or reach for some classic erotica like Anaïs Nin's *Little Birds* or Anne Rice's Sleeping Beauty trilogy. Let yourself go wherever you like. This is the safest, most private sex act in the universe. So own it. You can be the master or the slave. The stable boy or the estate owner. The movie star. The spy. Whoever doing whatever with whomever.

4. Take your time. A mental orgasm does not often come quickly or easily. And this pursuit should be far more about the journey than the destination. So stay with it as long as you like, and remember, there's no shame in ending with a little masturbation to finish the job if your mind needs some help!

The idea of having a mental orgasm is an interesting one. But honestly, what interests me even more is just how big of a role the mind plays in orgasm in general. I don't think we give it enough credit. Nor do I think that we take full advantage of its possibilities.

The mind is what can take you from zero to sixty. It is what can make the difference between coming and not, or between a so-so orgasm and an out-of-this-world one. It can be the answer to the question, "Why can I almost get there, but not quite get there?"

If you are committed to having the kind of orgasms that leave you unable to drive a motor vehicle, you have to get your mind involved. And this is not any sort of part-time gig. This is a full-time commitment.

You know those women who just exude sex? Who walk down the street and, whether you dig women sexually or not, make you think, "Damn. She is sexy"? I don't mean the super made-up, super self-conscious, super look-at-me, look-at-me women. I mean the women who are so much less concerned about what they wear and so much more concerned about being themselves, moving through the world with ease, and loving themselves and their bodies and their lives.

I know what you're thinking. I have a job. My house is a mess. My kids are climbing up the walls. I don't have time to be that girl sauntering down the street without a care in the world looking effortlessly sexy. But the thing is—you do. We only truly have power over one thing in this world—one—our minds.

You can wake up in the morning and say, *Ugh, life sucks, the world sucks, I'm fat, no one wants me. I don't have the time or the energy or the interest to have mind-blowing orgasms.* Or you can wake up and smile and arch your back into a giant stretch, roll your neck and give your thighs a quick massage and think about how lucky you are to be in a body that gives you pleasure. A body with soft warm skin and powerful muscles and delicious curves and shades of peach or brown or tan or yellow or pink or any color in between.

Still, easier said than done. I get it. But, remember, the question on the table is how you can find your best orgasm, your ultimate orgasm. And the answer is that there is no magic pill. There are skills and acts.

But there are also attitudes and mentalities, and these are the best place to start.

Throw out that ugly underwear. Get rid of those frayed sweats. I'm not saying you have to wear leather or lace. But make conscious choices about the things that touch your body and choose things that make you feel sexy, that make you feel beautiful, that make you feel powerful.

It may seem silly, or too easy, even. But think about how differently you feel about yourself depending on what you wear. There is no doubt in my mind that that feeling follows you all the way to the bedroom.

You may have to fake it till you make it, and that's okay. Think about how you want to feel about yourself, what will help you give yourself over in a way that will allow you to experience stellar sex, and the orgasms will follow.

Think about what you eat, how you carry yourself. Everything can up your sensory quotient if you want it to. I love to listen to a sexy playlist during the day, wear the kind of underwear that I know my girlfriend likes to see me in, eat fresh peaches, smell the rosemary as I walk into my sister's house. It might seem silly from the outside. But all of those things put me in my body and connect me to my senses, and that is what makes for a healthy, orgasmic life.

I also think about sex. A lot. Yes, it's part of my job. But even when it wasn't, I gave myself time during the day to imagine what was to come that night. A sexy frame of mind is what gives you that knowing look and that sexy swagger. You know those women you see who look so damn sexy, whether or not they have any of the Barbie-doll traits that we as a society mistake for sexiness? They are enjoying their bodies. They are letting their minds wander. They are smiling to themselves and maybe they're a little juiced up all day long about the orgasms in their future.

Call it goofy if you like. But that's the secret. That's the mind trick. That's the million-dollar answer to the million-dollar question. If you want to feel sexy, feel sexy. And if you can't yet, do whatever physical things will help you get there. Maybe it'll help you on your road to mental orgasm. But more likely, and more importantly to my mind, maybe it will help get you those killer orgasms that you long for. The clit is an amazing thing. More nerve endings than you could dream up. But the brain is the workhorse. So work it.

Many of the women I surveyed asked why some women just don't seem able to orgasm at all, no matter what. "Is it just a mental block?" they asked, and "Are they truly unable to orgasm? Why do many women have problems being able to just let go and feel secure and desired?"

Well, it is certainly possible to have a physical problem that would not allow a woman to have an orgasm. But it is far more possible that the issue has to do with shame or trauma. Shame about one's body is a huge issue. As is shame about sex in general, mostly due to sex-negative religious cultures.

If the issue is about your body, that may be bigger than we can tackle here. But I will tell you this. Your body is amazing. It can do the most incredible things. If you are playing alone, you deserve pleasure. So masturbate. Take care of yourself. If you're with a partner, that person is there for a reason. Don't second-guess them; they love your body, let them. If your weight is a health issue, think about making some healthy changes that will make you feel better about the body you live in.

If the issue is trauma, seek professional help. Sexual trauma is devastating. But it doesn't have to be the end of your sex life. It can be very hard to tackle this issue alone. Don't be afraid to seek help. It's not going to be easy. But it will definitely be easier than having to deal with such issues all by yourself. Things can only get better if you take the steps to make them better.

The brain-body connection is intricate and inextricable and impossible to remove from the orgasm equation. Of course, why would you want to, anyway? The brain has the power to move you from unaroused to about to explode. All you have to do is engage it.

In a universe where you are basically never unplugged from the outside world, let alone from your own brain, it can be hard to make the mental space needed to allow yourself the deepest possible orgasm exploration. But it's just like anything else: If you give it the time and focus it deserves, you will be rewarded richly for your efforts.

Your brain is at your service. A wandering one can work against you. So, take advantage of what it can do and allow it to work *for* you instead.

BEGINNING TO HEAL SEXUAL TRAUMA

Dealing with sexual trauma is a massive topic far too big to handle here. But I wanted to include these words from Staci Haines's book *Healing Sex*, which is an excellent resource for addressing sexual trauma.

Childhood sexual abuse teaches you to disregard your own internal sense of boundaries and to run your life by somebody else's rules. When you were abused, you did not get the opportunity to act on your internal sense of consent. You were not invited to state your boundaries, and if you managed to express your feelings, you were not heard or respected.

Sexual abuse can also have the effect of turning consent upside down and inside out. "No" meant "yes," and "yes" meant "no." Saying "no" had no effect or may have brought on worse abuse. You may have been manipulated into asking for sexual contact. Sexual contact may have been your only source of comfort or connection.

It is vital that you reintegrate the experience of choice and consent into your sex life. Regarding your body and soul, you are now the one who decides. You know have the first, middle, and last word on what you choose sexually. (Haines 2007, 105)

Visions of where we are going are always out in front of us. As we attain one goal, a new one stretches ahead to draw us onward. As you progress in healing, your ideas about your new sexuality will change. A new dream may emerge. Or you may realize midstream that what you thought you wanted isn't really what you want anymore. Your vision will change and grow over time.

What will your empowered sexual self look, sound, and feel like? (Haines 2007, 239)

Because You Asked

ONE OF MY FAVORITE parts of the survey I did for this book was hearing your questions about female orgasm. To be sure I answered all of them, I decided to include this mailbag chapter. So here it is, dedicated to you and all of your inspiring curiosity!

1. How can I achieve an orgasm during oral sex?

First of all, you don't have to. So don't feel pressured. But if you do want to do your best to get there, there are a few things to keep in mind. First, time. It can take thirty to forty-five minutes, on average, for a woman to orgasm via oral sex. Second, consider adding penetration. Fingers or a toy, vibrating or otherwise, can really help get you over the edge. (OhMiBod's Cuddle is one of my faves for this!) Third, anal penetration or pressure on your perineum can definitely help, which your partner can provide by pressing a fist into the space between your pussy and your anus. Fourth, position is key. Try placing a pillow or a wedge (Liberator makes an awesome one) under your bottom to give your partner's neck a break. Or, sit on her face so you can rub your pussy all over her mouth and nose to get perfect pressure in the perfect place.

In other words, listen to your body. Your body knows what it wants, when, and where. All you have to do is follow its lead!

2. Is it wrong to have too many orgasms when your partner only has one? Why can some women (like me) continue coming for hours, yet others can barely have one? How much is too much?

I love this three-parter because it addresses the thing that many women worry about: that somehow they are greedy little orgasm hoarders wanting more than their share. That's the great thing about orgasms. The more you have, the more you can have. We are each responsible for our own orgasms. And there are more than enough to go around. If your partner begrudges you even one orgasm, he or she knows how to show him or herself out. So, no, it's not wrong to have multiple orgasms when your partner only has one, unless you are somehow forcing your partner to have only one while you have many. Unless that's part of some mutually agreed-upon sex game, cut it out.

Why do women differ in their capacity for orgasm? Why indeed. All women's bodies are built differently. Couple that with our backgrounds and experiences and skills—learned and innate—and knowledge, and there is going to be some orgasm disparity. If you are a constant repeat comer, enjoy. If you're not, don't sweat it. Relish the ones you have, and if you want to work toward multiples—though this is not a requirement by any means—check out Chapter Nine in this book, about doing just that.

As for how much is too much, it depends. Are you going to work every day? Are you taking care of your responsibilities? Are you seeing to your loved ones? If you're holed up with an arsenal of toys and can't stop to eat or sleep or open the mail, we have a problem. But if your sexual adventures are a part of a balanced, happy life, then there's no reason to not enjoy orgasm after orgasm every chance you get. You're not going to break anything. In fact, the more orgasms you have, the more your body is primed for additional orgasms. So don't give a second thought to riding the orgasm train for as long as you can happily handle it.

3. *Is hours-long tantric orgasm a myth?*

I haven't experienced one. And I don't know anyone personally who has. But I wouldn't doubt that someone, somewhere may have enjoyed such an experience. When it comes to things like this, I find it hard to simply say, "No way. That's crazy." Because who knows?

4. *Why don't I have orgasms from intercourse alone, and how can I achieve that?*

What's wrong with me that I need clitoral stimulation?

How can I come without clitoral stimulation or toys?

How do I have an orgasm with a partner?

Sometimes I feel bad for my partner that I supplement his penetration with self (manual) stimulation, and I just wonder, is that really necessary or have I just gotten into a habit?

How common is it for heterosexual women to have a vaginal orgasm during regular vaginal intercourse?

I know many women do not come from internal stimulation and need clitoral stimulation to fully orgasm. Myself included. Internal still feels good and can be a turn-on, but I won't fully orgasm. Is this just biologically set in stone, or can I work to try and achieve orgasms both ways?

And that's just a handful of versions of this question I received. The pattern is not surprising, but that doesn't make it any less upsetting. This is mostly straight women, naturally. But it is also a question I get from lesbians who feel as if it is some sort of insult to touch themselves or to grab a vibrator and pitch in while having sex with their partner.

This is a huge issue and one I have touched on throughout the book. But I want to be really clear here, because this is a game-changer.

There is no right way to come.

There is no prize for coming without clitoral stimulation.

Most women need clit stim to come.

The blended orgasm is the best orgasm.

PVI is the least effective and least common way for women to orgasm.

This is all about biology, my friends. All of the juicy nerve endings are in your clit. The clit is so much more than the little (or not-so-little) nub you see on the outside. It is an entire internal system with dangling legs. Stretch out the clitoral legs, and you've got a part of the anatomy that's as long as any penis. That is why some women come from being penetrated. That clitoral system is being stimulated. So no matter how you look at it, orgasm is fundamentally based on clit stim.

Because of the way most women's bodies are built and because of the number of nerve endings in that marvelous little nub, most women need stimulation directly on said nub in order to come. Period. End of sentence. We have been made to believe that there is something wrong with us if we can't come from a few thrusts. That's just a load of bunk, and it's time to let it go.

Partners—no matter how close we are to them—are not mind readers. Women's bodies and desires are all different. So there is no need to feel bad about asking for what you want. And there is no reason not to lend a hand. What you see in the movies—porn and otherwise—is all show and is *all* about male ego. A partner who is truly interested in your pleasure will not be intimidated or put off by what you need to make you come. He will be interested only in making you come.

We have to let go of this old model: Man climbs on top. Man thrusts for three minutes till he comes. Woman is filled with ecstasy. Wrong. Delete. Forget that. Talking to your partner may not seem easy. But it is well worth it considering that the other option is faking it for the rest of your life. Forget that. And to hell with the male ego. If a man's world revolves around his thrusting being able to make you come, than he is a sad excuse for a man and you don't need him.

The same goes if you have a female partner, of course. This is about your orgasm, and your orgasm happens how and when and where you say and with whom and what you choose. No one "makes" you come. You come. How you get there has to do with your body and your mind, and any woman or man who thinks that she or he has any right to that is dead wrong. Dead wrong. Ego is the number-one orgasm killer.

This is a lot about body politics and sexual philosophy, I realize. So, for a more scientific take, I put this question to Dr. Joanna Ellington, an internationally recognized scientist in the area of sexual medicine, and asked if there is actually any scientific or medical problem with a woman needing clitoral stimulation in order to come.

She explained that the number-one issue with women not coming during PVI is, quite simply, the penis not being in the vagina long enough to facilitate orgasm. In addition, she says, "Women are not getting the right pressure on their entire clitoral/arousal tissue complex. It needs to include a mix of entry and deep stimulation, as well as grinding and stimulation of the glans (the most innervated area). On top is the best position (in studies) for female orgasm. She needs to play with movement and not have him force any rhythm or depth. She needs to choose the motion and he needs to last until she figures it out."

It's also really important to be fully aroused before PVI. Better yet, have at least one orgasm before penetration play (from a penis or a strap-on) becomes a part of the game. Reading dirty stories, watching dirty movies, talking dirty to one another; all of this can help up your game. Ellington also suggests using a lubricant. Not being wet enough can cause the kind of pain that does not lead to orgasms.

There really is only one way to have great orgasms—explore what gives you great orgasms without concern for hurting a partner's ego or guilt for having healthy sexual desire. Ask for it. Do it. Come.

5. How do I train my body to accept full pleasure? There are times when my boyfriend wants to do more, but I can't take it because I'm too sensitive.

Your orgasm is about your pleasure. So it doesn't matter if your partner wants to do more. If you're done, you're done. If you have a desire to continue pleasuring your partner, you can offer that option if he is not ready to stop. But if your body is done he *must* accept that without whining or begging. If he can't, well, you know the drill.

6. What do people like about orgasms?

I decided to tackle this question because it made me realize that some people, particularly those who have either never had an orgasm or never had a particularly good orgasm, might wonder about the reason for all the fuss, the writing, the research, the search for bigger, better, longer, ultimate.

Orgasm is the world's best, all-natural high. The ultimate ones, I mean. It's better than any exercise or adventure high I've ever experienced. They take me out of my body, out of my head, and into a place that I can only describe as pure bliss. I don't hear or see or feel anything but pleasure. Everything seems perfect and good and happy and, yes, I realize I sound like some sort of rainbows and unicorns and kitties kind of goofball. But it's true.

There are very few times in life when such joy interrupts our daily lives, and this is one we can access almost any time we like, by ourselves, no equipment required.

That's what people like about orgasms.

7. Why are some women unable to orgasm?

I decided it was best to turn to a professional for the reasons women might have difficulty orgasming. So I asked Dr. Ellington. Here's her take:

- *Operator error: Women in same-sex relationships orgasm at about twice the rate of women with men. Women know how to touch other women and where.*

- *Equipment failure: Size matters—women in partnerships with men with "large" penises more regularly orgasm through PVI (60 percent versus 35 percent). Staying power matters—orgasm from PVI is correlated to duration of PVI, not to foreplay. [Men] lasting longer allows women to come. Erectile dysfunction drugs that make the penis harder, longer, and wider [in] girth improves orgasm rate in women.*

- *Pharmacology: Hormonal contraceptives (such as the pill) decrease sexual response rates. SSRI antidepressants (which up to 25 percent of women in some age groups are on) greatly decrease arousal and orgasmic capacity. Narcotics, marijuana, steroids, [and] statins all decrease testosterone and sexual responsiveness.*

- *Biology: Sex steroid levels play a large role in orgasmic responsiveness. Women vary in their natural levels. Menopausal women without hormone replacement therapy have very low testosterone levels. Women with attractive men (as rated by independent third parties) have higher orgasm rates. Women who start having sex at a younger age orgasm more readily.*

- *Psychology: Women with higher perceived relationship quality (that is, women who feel they are in happy, healthy, satisfying relationships) have higher PVI orgasm rates. It is hard to be chronically mad at someone and have great sex. Women experience desire after being aroused. Men are aroused and then desire to have sex. Women often don't jump on the times they feel aroused to let it lead to desire and "readiness"—after reading the novel, or seeing the sexy film. Poor body image—women stress about body image to [the] detriment of getting turned on.*

In other words, lots of reasons, lots of solutions. The most important thing is that you ask the question. Your body should be able to orgasm. If it can't, you have a right to know why and an obligation to try to resolve the issue to the best of your ability.

8. *Why is female anatomy so baffling to men, and how can I encourage a partner to learn my trigger spots?*

Because female sexuality is such a powerful thing, it has been kept under wraps since, well, forever. We don't talk about it and share it and teach it and revel in it the way we should, and so many, many men are very, very much in the dark.

Show him. Take off your clothes. Spread your legs and show him. Teach him what's going on between your legs and show him what you do and don't like. This applies to women, too. If you haven't shown her what to do and she's not getting you off, you have no one to blame but yourself.

There is no prize for guessing. You're not a better lover if you didn't have to read the instructions or go through the tutorial first. The guys

I know who are the best in bed had a woman in her thirties show them the ropes when they were eighteen or nineteen. It's not a mystery why men don't know anything about women's bodies—no one tells them, and they're made to feel ashamed if they ask.

Well, that's just foolishness.

Show him. Tell him. Teach him.

Believe me, you'll both be glad you did.

9. I feel as if I developed my sexuality around the power and the turn-on I felt from my ability to give pleasure to a man. Rather than having this result in me being more in my body and ready to receive pleasure, it took me totally out of my body and completely focused on giving pleasure without a trust in my ability to receive it. How do you honor the pleasure of giving while simultaneously cultivating the ability to be in your body and receive pleasure?

I love this question because I relate to this question. Women are natural givers. It's our nature. But in some ways, not receiving is as selfish an act as not giving, because if we can't receive, then we are withholding ourselves from our partners.

So while it might seem like some sort of honorable, selfless act to fake orgasm or to forgo orgasm instead of asking for what you want or lending a hand, it's actually an incredibly selfish act not to allow your partner the same pleasure they are granting you—the pleasure to please.

This all has to do with self-worth and feeling valuable enough to receive pleasure. It can be easy to dismiss our sexual needs as women, because society at large does such a great job at shaming us for our desires.

In order to cultivate the ability to receive and truly enjoy pleasure, we have to first see ourselves as worthy. We have to see our bodies as worthy. We have to see our desire as worthy.

The best way to do that is to get to know your body. Masturbate. Admire the pleasure your body can enjoy. Take care of your body. Whatever that means to you. Do the things that make you feel good about it. Exercise it. Fuel it. Groom it. Dress it. Do the things from which you derive pleasure.

Many of us feel worthy when it comes to our minds, but still can't come to that same place of worthiness when it comes to our bodies and their pleasure.

This is about changing your mindset. Your partner deserves pleasure and your partner deserves to give you pleasure. If you can't do it for yourself right out of the gate, then do it for your partner first, and before you know it, you'll be able to do it for no other reason than that it's your right to receive pleasure.

Sex should be an amazing circular play of pleasure being given and received, with no end but sheer exhaustion or the demands of the outside world intruding. There is no foreplay. PVI is not the main event. No one's orgasm is more important than anyone else's. Sex must be mutual, consensual, and pleasurable. Those are the only things it must be. The rest is up to you and those with whom you choose to play.

10. How "normal" I am compared to others?

I wanted to end this chapter with this one because it's perfect. You are normal. Nothing about you is not normal. No matter how you seek pleasure, there's a 99.9 percent chance that there's another woman who likes what you like. We're all so very different. But one thing I have discovered from all of my research is that we're also all so strikingly similar.

You are normal and your body is normal and your pleasure is normal. The best piece of sex advice I could possibly give is this: Let it go. That's it. Let. It. Go. Your body is amazing. Orgasm is yours for the taking. Your sexuality is normal and wonderful, and it belongs to you. And if anyone or anything is telling you otherwise, it's time to say good riddance, because shame has no place in this conversation and there's no need to harbor any around the question of normalcy.

You are normal. Trust me. One woman in the survey says that all she wanted to know was that "It's okay to have orgasms the way I have them, and that there are no 'right' or 'wrong' ways to have them."

Now you know.

Discovering Your Ultimate Orgasm

My Personal Orgasm Project (P.O.P.)

I KNOW WHAT YOU'RE thinking. This is all well and good. But how am I going to actually find my ultimate orgasm?

Well, what I can tell you is how I found mine.

I started looking.

I didn't think it was missing, to be honest. I thought the orgasms I was having were perfectly fine, and as far as anything else went, I either wasn't capable or I wasn't interested in messing with it. What was the point?

But I realized I was being sloppy when it came to attending to my sexuality. I deserved more than just good orgasms. I owed it to myself to find my ultimate orgasm—and it was the best kind of research a girl could ask for. Yes, I did have to face some fears and some shame. I lost one partner and took a big risk on another. But that's the only way we learn and grow. And what's the point of being alive if we aren't actively engaged in learning and growing?

Female orgasm is a tricky, loaded subject. Even the experts have a habit of arguing about female orgasm. Why? Well, it's as mysterious as it isn't. We know that women generally find pleasure in having their clitoris stimulated. Ugh, I hate how that sentence sounds. And it took forever to craft it without it sounding dreadfully lawyerly and formal. That's the thing. It's tough to come up with a blanket statement about all female orgasm. Science keeps trying to figure it out. But I figure, instead of trying to figure it out in an effort to gain some sort of answer uniformity, why not just say the hell with finding an answer and instead agree to keep exploring, and who knows what we'll discover? That sounds like way more fun to me.

So if there are no answers, why the heck did I even bother to write this book? Well, think of it as a guidebook. I've tried to give you a better understanding of the terrain and what's been discovered, in hopes that you might want to start a little P.O.P. of your own. You know that saying about how it's not the destination, it's the journey? Nowhere is that more apropos than when it comes to orgasm.

A P.O.P. is something most of us need, whether we realize it or not. Why? Because orgasm fuels women, and it's our right and our responsibility to have the best ones possible.

The best P.O.P.s start with taking a look at where you are now. And there is no time like the present to take an orgasm assessment. So set aside some time, grab a pen and paper, and do your own orgasm assessment.

Orgasm Assessment

Where are you now?

How do you feel about your orgasms?

Are you having as many orgasms as you would like?

Are you having the type and strength of orgasms that you desire?

If you have a partner, have you talked to your partner about where you are now in terms of orgasms?

Are you masturbating regularly?

Are you satisfied with the orgasms you have when you masturbate?

Where do you want to be?

How do you want to feel about your orgasms?

How many orgasms would you like to be having daily? Weekly? Monthly?

What type and strength of orgasms do you desire?

If you have a partner, do you want to be able to talk to your partner about your orgasms?

How often do you want to be masturbating?

What would you qualify as satisfying when it comes to the orgasms you have when you masturbate?

How are you going to get there?

Who do you need to reach your orgasm goals?

Are you prepared to commit to your orgasm goals? Mentally? Physically? Time-wise?

If you have a partner, is your partner committed to you achieving your orgasm goals?

Next Steps

So what do you do now? Start here.

Refuse to check the boxes

As a society, we have a lousy habit of wanting everything to fit in tidy little boxes. Female orgasm is not going to let anyone put it in a box—or a corner, for that matter!

Try and try again

The truth is that female orgasm isn't about finding the magic spot. Just as losing weight isn't about some secret fruit in the forests of the Amazon or a secret pill in the depths of a lab. Female orgasm is about discussing all of the places from which an orgasm can emanate and discovering how that can happen.

Talk to your friends

I understand that it can be hard to know what to do or how an orgasm can or should feel unless you have some way of gauging or comparing it. Women experience orgasm differently, but the ones who are having really good ones report a lot of similarities.

Talk to your partner

This isn't easy, I'll admit, especially if you've been doing things the same way for a long time and they're "fine" or, at least that's what you tell yourself and your partner. It can be equally challenging to talk to a new partner. What if your partner judges you or you scare your partner off?

Regardless of the challenge, the conversation is always worth it. It saves you both from having to guess or hide your true desires. And as Schell says, "A fulfilling sexual relationship revolves around the discovery of what you both want and the conveyance of these assorted desires" (*The Guide to Lesbian Sex,* 95).

In an effort to talk about just what those things might be, here's a fun list to use to start talking to your partner about your interests and desires. You may want to print out this list and note how you feel about each. "Interested but scared." "No way." "Yes, please!" Or something like that. Then compare lists and see where the common ground is. That's a great place to start!

Lap dance
Public sex
Filming your escapades
Bondage
S&M
Dirty talk
Fisting
Oral sex
Analingus
Dominance & Submission
Gender play
Threesomes/Group sex/Sex clubs/Sex parties
Masturbation
Sexting/Phone sex/Video sex
Quickies
Role playing/Fantasy
Rough play

Sensory deprivation

Spanking

Striptease

Toys

Voyeurism

Why Now?

To my mind, sexy is as sexy does. If you want a more orgasmic life, then live more orgasmically. Cut out the things that don't add to your sensuality quotient and add in the things that do. Sure, we all have to wash the dishes. But why not buy a dishwashing soap with a swoonworthy fragrance? Sure, you have to fold the laundry. But there's nothing saying you can't do it in your underwear while swaying your hips to Sade's "By Your Side."

I get it. Believe me. The world has a hold on you and you simply can't be bothered with finding your ultimate orgasm. It's too much trouble. Takes too much time. It's just not important enough. You have sex once in a while. The sex is fine. Sometimes it's even good. You love your partner, you don't want to rock the boat. You have a job to go to, bills to pay, kids to raise. You don't have the time or the energy anymore for making out in the kitchen or slow dancing in the living room or lying back and letting your partner thrill you.

Let me bother you with an old story. It's about a man who cut down trees for a living. On the first day, he cut down one hundred trees. On the second day, only eighty. On the third, sixty. And it wasn't long before he could hardly cut but a handful down. He told his neighbor of his troubles, and his neighbor said, "When was the last time you sharpened your saw?" The man just looked at him and shook his head. "I haven't got the time," he replied.

If your orgasmic life is lagging, it's likely that other things are suffering in your life—your relationships, your general joy in life, your work; everything, really. If you think you don't have time to work on orgasm, think again. The real question is—do you have enough time to *not* work on it?

The answer is no, and the time is now.

Orgasm is important. It's vital. It's the center of our power, and we have to tend to it, and we have to partner with people who support and nurture that tending and who are committed to our being wholly orgasmic beings.

We make over our bodies, our kitchens, our wardrobes. Surely we deserve an orgasm makeover as much as or more than we deserve those makeovers.

Remember those "Choose Your Own Adventure" books? All throughout the text you could determine what road to take, what dragon to slay, what door to enter, what person or equipment to bring along.

This is your own, real-life, choose your own adventure. You get to choose who you want to be, who you want to play with, and what you want to bring along with you.

What's Behind Every P.O.P.

Social expectations of sex are limited to male pleasure. And that can bleed into lesbian relationships, too, where either or both partners demur to the other's orgasm. "No, you come." "No, you come." No. You both can come. You both will come. Everyone will come if we make the shift from orgasm to ultimate orgasm. If we each do a P.O.P. of our own and find what works for us, even if it's scary and surprising and new.

The purpose of sex is mutual pleasure. I don't go in and say, "I'm going to sit on your face because that gives me pleasure, and when I come, we're done, and if you come while I'm doing that, that would be super." And yet when PVI is the foregone conclusion, that's exactly what's happening. When a woman has sex with a man, his orgasm is never in question. Hers always is. The mindset should be "We're here to come." Emphasis on the *we*.

There can't be any assumptions. As a woman, I don't know what will make you come, and I don't assume that making myself come will make my partner come. But men generally do make that assumption when it comes to having sex with women, and it's highly problematic.

When you have a conversation with someone who you are going to engage with sexually, you can use the language of your P.O.P. and enthusiastic consent and ultimate orgasm and blended orgasm to have that conversation. What are the goals of sex? What are the goals of orgasm? This is not about giving or taking blame. It's about talking about what you need in order to achieve your ultimate orgasm.

How does woman-positive, heterosexual sex look? It's consensual. It's mutual. It's pleasure-seeking. It's without rules. It's without *shoulds* and is instead about *what ifs*.

It seems like every decade or so, a feminist comes along and says, Vaginal orgasm is a myth. PVI intercourse is about men. Heterosexual sex is too male-focused. Well, it's time to say it again, and if women want full equality, from the boardroom to the bedroom, it's time for all of us to really take heed this time.

It's imperative that you invest in the things that improve your life and divest all the things that are sucking the joy from it. The time and work required to do that may seem daunting. But what you get in return will be at least tenfold greater than the effort you put in.

If you think cleaning up clutter is difficult, try living in it forever.

If you think breaking up is too hard, imagine living with that person forever.

If you think changing how you treat your body's health isn't worth the trouble, try surviving in a body you have ignored.

If you think rewriting that negative loop in your head is too daunting, try existing in a mental state of constant self-critique and self-bullying.

It's time to let go. It's time for every woman's P.O.P. Imagine what the energy would be like if every woman were enjoying ultimate orgasms. Amazing. Let's get started.

P.O.P. Positions for Play

Here are some of my favorite lesbian positions for discovering your ultimate orgasm with a partner: "(many of which can be easily tweaked for heterosexual couples)

1. Have your partner sit between your legs. This is as basic as it gets. But it gives your partner a full view and access to your pussy, ass, and breasts.

2. Sit on your partner's lap with your legs on either side of her. You can look into each other's eyes and kiss to your heart's content, and your partner can reach around your back and slide her fingers inside you from behind. You can rub your clit on her, or you can lift your pelvis up a little so she can rub your clit.

3. Lie on your back on top of your partner with your knees bent. Have her thread her legs through yours in order to keep your legs spread. Have her slap your pussy. (Try it. You might like it.) This way, she can masturbate you the way she masturbates herself. It's a great way to get off and let her learn your style. (If you like to role play, a few throaty *no*'s while she reminds you how wet you're getting and continues to slap you can do the trick.)

4. Lie on your stomach with your legs spread and have your partner straddle one of your legs. She can rub her clit on your leg. Then have her finger you while you rub against a vibrator positioned beneath you, on your clit.

5. Have your partner kneel. Straddle one of her knees. She can finger you from behind and you can rub your clit against her thigh.

6. Lie right on top of your partner and rub your clit against hers (or vice versa!).

7. Straddle her face. There is nothing like giving your partner full access to your naughty bits while giving you the leverage and control to grind your pussy to orgasm.

Meanwhile, you can reach back and finger her pussy.

8. Have your partner lie with her legs spread and one knee up. Scissor yourself into her so that you can hold onto her knee for leverage.

9. Lie on your back. Using a G-Zone vibrator like OhMi-Bod's Cuddle with the tip curving up, have her penetrate you using downward pressure. Have her mix it up by moving the vibrator from side to side inside you. Then you can stimulate your clit manually or with a vibrator.

10. Sixty-nine is a fun but challenging position. It's fun for obvious reasons. It's challenging because having an orgasm involves focus. So being distracted by also giving someone an orgasm can be tricky. But don't fret. There's no need to come at the same time. Enjoy the play and follow the orgasm that seems to be getting to the finish line first. Then you can circle back and finish the other person off!

11. Get down on your forearms and knees and have your partner enter you from behind with a vibrator, dildo, strap-on, or her fingers. You can use a vibrator on your clit as well, or you can grind into the bed or your partner's thigh.

P.O.P. Tools

As long as we're discussing a few of my favorite things, here are my favorite toys and equipment for discovering your ultimate orgasm.

1. Betty Dodson's Vaginal Barbell—I don't know what the deal is with this thing. But there's something about its weight and smooth texture and bumps and ridges that makes it an amazing tool for partner sex and masturbation.

2. Liberator wedge—Leverage is everything. Getting in the right position can make all the difference between coming and not coming, or between an average orgasm and an ultimate one.

3. OhMiBod Cuddle—This curved G-Zone vibrator is ideal for partner play or masturbation, and it's great for penetration and clit stim.

4. Jimmyjane Form 2—This is my go-to clit stim vibrator. It has an awesome soft, pliable texture and two bunny-like "ears" that you can position your clit in between for an out-of-this-world orgasm.

5. Lelo Mona Wave—This toy is great for G-Zone play.

6. Je Joue FiFi—The FiFi does a great job of hitting the G-Zone and the clit, and the texture is heavenly.

7. We-Vibe—This wearable toy is excellent for couples play when it comes to penetration, as it stimulates the external bud of the clit hands-free!

Your P.O.P.

If you take nothing else away from this book, I hope you'll take away the importance of being in the zone and the power of the blended orgasm. There are plenty of tips and tricks and zones and methods. But the truth is that there is simply no substitute for feeling sexy and confident and relaxed and entitled to pleasure.

There are lots of things you can do to feel more open to pleasure. Here are a few starter ideas:

1. Start with the assessment. Have your partner take it, too. Then work through the Practice section how-to's in Chapters 7 through 11. Try the positions. Seek out the zones. Spend some time with yourself. Play with your partner. This is your P.O.P., your chance to find your ultimate orgasm.

2. Eat sexy. For me, that means nothing greasy or fried or heavy. But you have to find your own sexy food menu. Eat what makes your senses feel alive and your body feel charged up and ready to go.

3. Move sexy. That could mean walking or dancing or running. It could mean the gym or it could simply mean allowing your hips to sway at the grocery store. Having great orgasms is about being in your body, and movement is the best way to get connected with your body.

4. Play sexy. Watch woman-positive, sex-positive porn or other sexy TV or films. Read erotica like Rachel Kramer Bussel anthologies (including *Come Again: Sex Toy Erotica* and *Best Bondage Erotica 2015*), Anne Rice (including the Sleeping Beauty trilogy), or Anaïs Nin (including *Little Birds* and *Delta of Venus*). Sext with your partner or call and leave a suggestive voice message. Leave your partner a sexy note in her lunch, or pull him aside and give him a sneak peek of what he can get his hands on later. But no touching yet! Think about it. If you spend all day in a zero-sex zone, it's no wonder that it's hard to get your head in the game when the clock starts. But if there are little teases or reminders throughout the day, it will be a heck of a lot easier to slip right into your happy place when the time is right.

5. Start your day with an orgasm and notice your skin, your mood, the way people respond to you. End your day with an orgasm and take note of how you fall asleep and what (if any) dreams you have or remember. Have an orgasm in the middle of the day. Notice how differently your day moves after you have it compared to before. This experiment is about consciousness. Even if it's forced consciousness at the beginning, it's a start—and a good one!

6. Talk dirty. Keep your eyes open. Kiss more. A lot more. Follow your pussy and not your head for a change. Ask for what you want. Settle for nothing less. Respect your own orgasm. Don't consent to sex that cares nothing for your orgasm. There are so many items on the menu, including oral sex, penetration, fingering or fisting, clit stim, anal

play, toys—all the good stuff we talked about herein.

7. Explore the zones. Remember, all of these zones and spots and ways to play are just menu items. You get to pick and choose and play and explore, and you can change your mind every time you play. You can even change your mind mid-play!

8. Keep this book in your nightstand. Carry it around. Share notes on it with your partner. Talk about it with your friends at book club. Let's change the paradigm. Let's make sex about pleasure. Let's up the ante.

9. Take the week-long "new to-do" challenge—try something new every day for a week. A new position. A new zone. A new game. Anything to reset your body and your mind.

10. Then take the one-week partnered orgasm challenge. In Chapter Five, I mentioned a one-week masturbation challenge. If you are partnered, I invite you to take this one-week partnered orgasm challenge as well. It doesn't matter what you do or when or where. All that matters is that you orgasm every day with a partner working with you to help you facilitate that orgasm. Check in with yourself throughout and after the week and see how you're feeling about yourself, your partner, and the world at large when you have orgasm in your life.

11. Talk to your partner. Talk to your friends. Talk to your family. Talk to a professional.

12. Learn about yourself. Masturbate. Know your body. Know what you like. Share that with your partner.

And Beyond

The only thing sexier than a woman who knows what she wants and asks for it is a woman willing to explore anything and everything in pursuit of her biggest O. Whenever women tell me that their sex life is flailing, I always ask them how they play. When they respond with a puzzled look, I ask them again.

"Play?" they say.

"Yes," I answer. "How do you play?"

"We don't play. We have sex."

That's when I know that what she is doing in bed has become routine. The exploration and excitement are gone, and now she is engaging in "Have you come yet?" sex, which is boring at best and downright depressing at worst.

I suggest that she mix it up. Do anything and everything but what she normally does. Take your sex script, rip it in half, and throw it out the window. No more doing what you always do. The only pursuit is pleasure the likes of which you have never before experienced but have always longed for.

Now, ask yourself this question: How would you and your partner play if mutual pleasure were the only focus?

Answer that and you will never bemoan a boring sex life again.

Answer that and you will find your sexual self.

Answer that and you will discover your ultimate orgasm.

Acknowledgments

THERE ARE SO MANY people I want to thank. First and foremost, I want to extend my deepest gratitude to my amazing publisher, Brenda Knight, who came to me with this idea and trusted me to run with it, supporting me, pushing me, and raising me up every step of the way. I want to thank all of the Cleis family as well who have been incredibly supportive from start to finish. Thank you Davey, Robin, Samantha, Julian, Sarah, Mia, and Kara for all of your unwavering patience with me and your incredible dedication to me and my work.

I also want to profusely thank my little sister, Rebecca Block, for the endless hours of support and talks and editing and organizing and restructuring and helping me to take this project from a pile of words and turn it into a real book.

I want to thank my dad, Ken Block, for the endless phone calls and pep talks and hash-out sessions. I also owe the deepest gratitude to Betty Dodson, my spiritual grandmother, who inspired and empowered me throughout this project.

Special thanks also to Jillian Eugenios, Tara McCoy, Amanda May, Jenn Brantmier, Janet Lynn Trevino, Rebekah Torres, E, Jude Schell, Dr. Joanna Ellington, Megan Andelloux, Carlin Ross, Noah Michelson, Dr. Beverly Whipple, Dr. Justin Garcia, and copyeditor extraordinaire, Elizabeth Smith.

And I want to profusely thank all the writers and researchers, both contemporary and those who came before me, for all of the books and essays and research and thinking that served as the foundation for my work. And I owe a great deal of thanks to the nearly 150 women who took the survey that I used when writing this book. Thank you, thank you, thank you.

Finally, I want to thank my amazing girlfriend, Lacey Brutschy, who has been so insanely supportive and generous and kind to me during this process, talking and experimenting and over-processing with me whenever and however and wherever I wanted and needed. I love you.

About the Author

JENNY BLOCK is a frequent contributor to a number of high-profile publications from *Huffington Post* to *Playboy*, and is the author of *Open: Love, Sex, and Life in an Open Marriage* (winner of a 2008 Lambda Literary Award). She appears regularly on HuffPo Live, the HuffPo Sex and Love Podcast, and is featured in HuffPo's first ever, free-standing multimedia project. She holds both her BA and her MA in English from Virginia Commonwealth University and taught college composition for nearly ten years.

Her work appears in and on a wide variety of publications and websites, including yourtango.com, American Way, Veranda, the Dallas Morning News, the Dallas Voice, edgedallas.com, literarymama.com, Spirit, chow.com, and ellegirl.com.

She is often called on as an expert on sex and women's sexuality for yourtango.com, bustle.com, *Woman's Day* magazine, sheknows.com, and many others.

Her essay "And Then We Were Poly" is included in Rebecca Walker's book, *One Big Happy Family: 18 Writers Talk About Polyamory, Open Adoption, Mixed Marriage, Househusbandry, Single Motherhood, and Other Realities of Truly Modern Love* (Riverhead Hardcover, 2009), which received a starred review from Kirkus. Jenny's essay "On Being Barbie" is included in the book *It's a Girl: Women Writers on Raising Daughters* (Seal Press, 2006).

Jenny has appeared on a variety of television and radio programs, including *Nightline, Fox and Friends, The Glenn Beck Show, The Tyra Banks Show, Good Morning Texas, The Morning Show with Mike and Juliet,* foxnews.com (online video), *Playboy Radio, The Alan Colmes Show, The Young Turks,* and BBC Radio.

Open: Love, Sex, and Life in an Open Marriage was written about or reviewed in and a variety of publications and sites, including *Publishers Weekly, Library Journal, Glamour, Marie Claire, Curve, Observer UK, Maxi* (Germany), *Psychologies* (UK), *Playgirl,* NPR's *Morning Edition, The New York Times,* feministing.com, *San Francisco Chronicle, New York Daily News, 2: The Magazine for Couples* (Canada), wow-womenonwriting.com, and the *Baltimore City Paper.*

Jenny has also spoken in bookstores and other venues all across the country, including the Wyly Theatre, the Texas Theater, Georgetown University, and the Science Museum of Virginia.

Photo credit: Steph Grant, www.stephgrantphotography.com

References

Blue, Violet. 2006. *The Adventurous Couple's Guide to Sex Toys*. Berkeley, CA: Cleis Press.

———. 2012. *The Smart Girl's Guide to the G-Spot*. Berkeley, CA: Cleis Press.

———. 2014. *Kissing: A Field Guide*. Berkeley, CA: Cleis Press.

———. 2014. *The Ultimate Guide to Sexual Fantasy*. Berkeley, CA: Cleis Press.

———. 2010. *The Ultimate Guide to Cunnilingus*. Berkley, CA: Cleis Press.

Castellanos, Madeleine. 2010. "Is the U-Spot a New Spot?" Good in Bed. http://www.goodinbed.com/blogs/sex_doctors/2010/12/is-the-u-spot-a-new-spot/

Chalker, Rebecca. 2011. *The Clitoral Truth*. New York: Seven Stories Press.

Dodson, Betty. 1987. *Sex for One: The Joy of Selfloving*. New York: Harmony.

Dodson, Betty. 2014. "A Woman's Erection Needs 20–30 Minutes of Adequate Clitoral Stimulation." http://dodsonandross.com/blogs/betty-dodson/2014/10/womans-erection-needs-20-30-minutes-adequate-clitoral-stimulation.

Garcia, J.R., E.A. Lloyd, K. Wallen, and H.E. Fisher. 2014. "Variation in Orgasm Occurrence by Sexual Orientation in a Sample of U.S. Singles." *Journal of Sexual Medicine*. doi: 10.1111/jsm.12669

Guttmacher Institute, Sex and STD/HIV education, State Policies in Brief, October 2011, http://www.guttmacher.org/statecenter/spibs/spib_SE.pdf, accessed Jul. 10, 2014.

Haines, Staci. 2007. *Healing Sex: A Mind-Body Approach to Healing Sexual Trauma*. San Francisco: Cleis Press.

Hawley, Patricia H. & William A. Hensley IV. 2009. "Social Dominance and Forceful Submission Fantasies: Feminine Pathology or Power?" *The Journal of Sex Research* 46(6): 568–585.

Jannini, Emmanuele A., Beverly Whipple, Sheryl A. Kingsberg, Odile Buisson, Pierre Foldès, and Yoram Vardi. 2010. "Who's Afraid of the G-Spot? Controversies in Sexual Medicine." *Journal of Sexual Medicine* 7:25–34

Jannini, Emmanuele A., Alberto Rubio-Casillas, Beverly Whipple, Odile Buisson, Barry R. Komisaruk, and Stuart Brody. 2012. "Female Orgasm(s): One, Two, Several." Controversies in Sexual Medicine. *Journal of Sexual Medicine*. 9:956–65.

Kaufman, Miriam, Cory Silverberg, and Fran Odette. 2007. *The Ultimate Guide to Sex and Disability*. San Francisco: Cleis Press.

Koedt, Anne. 1972. *Radical Feminism*. New York: Quadrangle.

Ladas, Alice Kahn, and Beverly Whipple. 1982. *The G Spot and Other Recent Discoveries about Human Sexuality*. New York: Holt, Rinehart, and Winston,

Newman, Felice. 1999. *The Whole Lesbian Sex Book*. San Francisco: Cleis Press.

Palmore EB. Predictors of the longevity difference: a 25-year follow-up. Gerontologist 1982; 22: 513-8.

Ryan, Christopher, and Cacilda Jethá. 2010. *Sex at Dawn: The Prehistoric Origins of Modern Sexuality*. New York: Harper Collins.

Schell, Jude. 2005. *The Guide to Lesbian Sex*. Irvington, NY: Hylas Publishing.

———. 2008. *Lesbian Sex: 101 Lovemaking Positions*. Berkeley, CA: Celestial Arts.

———. 2011. *Her Sweet Spot: 101 Sexy Ways to Find and Please It*. Berkeley, CA: Celestial Arts.

Sanders, S., Hill, B., Yarber, W., Graham, C., Crosby, R., Milhausen, R., (2010) "Misclassification bias: diversity in conceptualisations about having 'had sex,'" *Sexual Health*. 7(1), 31-34.

Sherfey, Mary Jane. 1972. *The Nature and Evolution of Female Sexuality*. New York: Random House.

Symons, D. 1979. *The Evolution of Human Sexuality*. New York: Oxford University Press.

Taormino, Tristan. 2006. *The Ultimate Guide to Anal Sex for Women*, 2nd ed. San Francisco, CA: Cleis Press.

Taormino, Tristan. 2012. *The Ultimate Guide to Kink*. Berkeley, CA: Cleis Press.